Lavidge

A common sense guide to professional advertising

No. 612
$9.95

Lavidge

A common sense guide to professional advertising

by Arthur W. Lavidge

TAB BOOKS
Blue Ridge Summit, Pa. 17214

FIRST EDITION

FIRST PRINTING—MAY 1973

Copyright ⊃1973 by Arthur W. Lavidge

Printed in the United States
of America

International Standard Book No. 0-8306-3612-9

Library of Congress Card Number: 72-81365

To the staff of Lavidge & Associates,
a great group of advertising professionals,
and particularly to Marghie and Pat without
whose assistance it could not have been done.

And to my family for their encouragement.

Acknowledgments:
Marghie Watson, Editorial assistance
Gary Haynes, Design and jacket
Stuart Eichel, Illustrations
House of Typography (Memphis), Headlines
Capper Inc. (Knoxville), Halftone engravings

Foreword

Anyone who has an interest in or a curiosity about advertising will enjoy this book. It is an especially valuable resource for the student and the young professional. And it is my opinion that the experienced hand cannot help but pick up some ideas that will aid him in his business.

The writer has done a rather remarkable job of condensing a lifetime of study, observations, and experience into a short, easy-to-read volume. The material is well documented and relevant to today's advertising practice.

After a quarter of a century in higher education — all in advertising, marketing, and communications — I can appreciate the enormous task involved in thoroughly researching, evaluating, and writing an important book such as this.

The final result is a significant contribution to the understanding of advertising procedures and effectiveness. It is a book that can be read and used by advertising people, students, and everyone in business.

Dean Donald C. Hileman, Ph.D.
College of Communications
University of Tennessee

About
The
Author

Arthur W. Lavidge is chairman and chief executive
officer of Lavidge & Associates Inc., one of the
Southeast's largest advertising agencies. His experience
encompasses all phases of advertising work. Today, the
company he heads represents many leading national,
regional, and local concerns.

Born in Chicago, Illinois, Lavidge graduated from
DePauw University where he captained the football
and baseball teams in his senior year. After serving as
a pilot in the U.S. Naval Air Corps during World War
II, he returned to Chicago where he took graduate
study in advertising at Northwestern University. After
three years in varying responsibilities with several
advertising companies, he opened an advertising agency
with a secondhand typewriter, a card table for a desk,
and no clients.

He has served as an instructor in marketing and
advertising at the University of Tennessee, and as an
instructor in salesmanship for several schools. He is a
contributing editor for Southern Advertising/Markets.
And, because of his extensive and diversified

experience is greatly in demand as a marketing consultant.

Married, with three children and a granddaughter, he spends such free time as he has pursuing his interests in travel and golf.

Contents

Introduction

This is a practical book. Within these pages you will find more useful information in three hours time than you normally could in three months at the library. The book is designed to be used, like a navigational chart, for direction in all phases of advertising responsibility. The contents are no substitute for talent. But talent, like ideas, must be effectively channeled. Advertising today is a vital part of the American way — first and foremost in business, but also in cultural activities, education, government, and all forms of mass communication.

Advertising is a controlled form of communicating. It is vital to the dissemination of ideas and useful information. It is free of editorial editing. To be resultful, advertising must be honest. The techniques of professional advertising have advanced rapidly in recent years. And with this has come increased opportunity for people interested in a career in this field.

Over the years I've had the experience of viewing advertising from almost every point of view. As a student, teacher, writer, media man, researcher, and agency executive. Some of the ideas expressed herein have been expressed before. They've become part of my thinking because experience has proven that they're practical, honest ideas that work. Other ideas — and opinions — are my own, also arrived at through experience. If the reader takes issue with one, some, or all of my ideas, so be it. I'd rather provoke thought than pontificate.

The book was written to serve four purposes.

First, to give the student an overview of the field and to introduce him to advertising fundamentals.

Second, to acquaint the young advertising man (or woman) with the essentials of his (or her) job, and with the essentials of others' jobs. In advertising, no man is an island. You mind other people's business as well as your own; when you understand the work of others, then you are able to see your responsibilities in a more meaningful perspective.

Third, to stimulate the old hand to think more about his own work and to learn more about the work of others.

And fourth, this book is for the benefit of the advertiser. It is intended to give him insight into advertising, to show him what he may expect from it, how each man performs, and how coordinated effort produces results for him. It is my conviction that taking the client "backstage" will be helpful to him and to his agency.

This is deliberately a short book, intended for reference and guidance. It's my hope that it will not just be read and shelved but *used*.

I
The advertising agency man

The Advertising Agency Man

Thousands know him. They've met him in novels, on the stage, and in the movies. He was a nice guy before he got into the ad game, but not now. His ideals are gone. He's chronically unhappy. Can't sleep at night. Drinks too much. Neglects his family and is a cynic and a hypocrite. But he has this conscience which finally gets to him. He leaves the agency and finds peace and happiness editing a weekly paper with a circulation of 500 in a little town in Maine where no one has ever heard of Madison Avenue. That's how it ends – the book, or the movie, or the play.

There's another advertising agency man. This is the one who is analyzed by economists, sociologists, and psychologists. He is not even a nice guy *underneath*. He's pictured as a Svengali who has hypnotized the public and made it his creature. It follows where he leads, does as he commands. Americans are under the influence of advertising, the critics claim. They have become bland, covetous; their only goals are comfort, wealth, and pleasure. In this age of washday miracles, spiritual values have gone down the drain with the grease and grime.

The ad man really is not all that bad, although, being human, he has his virtues and his vices. If he is a good and effective ad man, he doesn't consider advertising a force for good or evil because he understands it for what it is: a technique for selling. If advertising is a technique for selling, then the ad man is, primarily, a salesman.

This, of course, does not exempt the ad man from the obligation to be fair and honest in his dealings with the public. Advertising that is untruthful, advertising that deceives by greying the truth, and advertising that is banal, insistent, irritating, and in poor taste, does exist. But not for long. The public will not be hoodwinked and has only to try a product once to unmask sham and falsehood. The point is this: It is not the ad man's place to decide what the public *should* want; it is his place to find out what the public *does* want, specifically, from the product that he is selling. He then offers meaningful information about the product to the public, information that answers the question, "What can this product (or service) do for me?"

Advertising as a Technique for Selling

Advertising is a substitute for, or an aid to, personal selling. The ad man is a salesman who doesn't call on his customers, but who speaks to them instead through the media of mass communication: newspapers, magazines, TV, radio, outdoor posters, and direct mail. Or, by preconditioning the prospects, he may pave the way for personal selling.

The ad man, like the personal salesman, uses the psychology of selling to win a favorable reaction for his product. People are, by nature, wary of anyone who wants to sell them something, and they may pride themselves on sales resistance. Their attitude is "Go on, try to sell me, if you can." They may suspect that the salesman, by fast talking or sly persuasion, is trying to put something over on them.

The salesman, therefore, must understand his prospect. He must put himself in the prospect's shoes. He must know him — what kind of person he is, how he lives, what he needs, what he wants. The salesman must have empathy with him, understand him, and involve him in the selling experience. Until he is involved, the prospect cannot be convinced that the salesman is interested in him and can help him. To win a favorable response, the salesman must speak to the prospect in his own language and set the product in a frame of reference related to the prospect's life experiences.

Like any good salesman, the ad man knows that overstatement will frighten the prospect away. He also knows that he is not selling his own talents or his own pleasing personality. He knows that advertising must stay close to real people, to real situations, and that it must be tied to the product itself. Otherwise it will not sell.

In the advertiser-agency relationship, *the agency should be the expert on the customer, the advertiser the expert on the product*. In this context, the ad man represents not the manufacturer (whose interests are not necessarily those of the customer), but the public. The ad man knows what the public wants from the manufacturer's product, and he knows what features of the product are most appealing to the public and most likely to prompt a purchase.

As the advertiser and the agency work together, this relationship undergoes a metamorphosis. The advertiser becomes more expert on the public; the agency more expert on the product. When this occurs, they more effectively complement each other in their respective areas of primary responsibility.

Two Primary Objectives

The ad man simplifies his approach to the ad task by thinking in terms of advertising's two primary objectives – *share of mind* and *share of market*. Let's start our discussion of these objectives with a basic, stripped-down definition of each.

> *Share of mind* refers to the number of people who *prefer* the brand.
> *Share of market* refers to the number of people who actually *buy* the product.

Before the ad man can determine the relative weight of each primary objective in his advertising campaign, he must first know the sales objective. The sales objective may be to increase *share of market* from 5% to 10% (an ambitious objective!). Advertising will be one part of the total marketing mix which will bear on this objective.

The importance of advertising's role will vary, depending on the product and how it is sold. In the case of an industrial product, the role of advertising might be to produce inquiries for follow-up by the company's salesmen. In the case of life insurance, it might be to condition consumer attitudes so that when the agent calls there will be a higher degree of acceptance than existed before the advertising appeared. In the case of a package goods item, it is to move the product off the retailer's shelf and into the consumer's shopping cart.

In the instance of the industrial product, the objective is a favorable *share of mind* resulting in an inquiry. In the instance of life insurance, it is a favorable *share of mind*. In the instance of the package goods item, it is a favorable *share of mind* and a specific *share of market*.

In other words, the sales objective will make a great difference in how the ad man tells his product's story. Is advertising to be the salesman, as it is for most package goods, or is it to pave the way for the salesman by acting as a conditioning agent? One cosmetics company uses advertising to prepare the prospect for the salesman. This is *share of mind* advertising. Another cosmetics company uses *share of mind* advertising to win the prospect's acceptance and *share of market* advertising to move the prospect into the store.

To expand our definition: *share of mind* refers to the number of people who remember the message and, as a result, have some degree of preference for the brand. The *share of mind* objective is for the message to be made as memorable as possible to the greatest possible number of logical prospects for the product.

The "Fly the Friendly Skies" campaign for United Airlines typifies *share of mind* advertising. The prospect may not immediately book a seat on a flight, but as he is exposed to the campaign over a period of time, a pleasing picture of the airline forms in his mind — flying with this airline would be safe, comfortable, convenient, and fun.

We see, then, that *share of mind* advertising arouses interest, communicates ideas, gains acceptance, builds confidence, and predisposes the public to buy. It wins friends and influences people by building a pleasing image of the product or service.

Share of market advertising is a more urgent technique than *share of mind* advertising. The latter aims to instill in prospects a favorable attitude toward the product, while the former aims specifically at getting people to buy the product.

Let's go back to our example. As the airline wins increasing *share of mind*, they will see it convert into increasing *share of market*. But the airline wants to accelerate sales *now*. What can be done? The airline looks for a way to increase traffic and notes the mobility of the American businessman. Why should his wife be grounded, left standing forlornly at the airport, watching her husband's plane vanish into the airline's "friendly skies"?

"TAKE ME ALONG," says the ad, "or how to turn your husband's next business trip into a swinging time for both of you." A great idea. Why not? Too expensive? Not at all! The airline will offer a "Take Me Along" fare "that saves you up to one-third of a wife's fare, with our credit card that lets you charge it." Two strong incentives are presented in the campaign, one psychological ("How long has it been since you danced together? Explored a city together? Or been alone together?"), the other financial. And in each ad the general theme, "Fly the Friendly Skies of United," is reiterated to call up the favorable _share of mind_ image in the minds of prospects.

This is not to say, of course, that _share of mind_ advertising should not sell products or that _share of market_ advertising should not build confidence. But the ad man keeps in mind that in order to have a really healthy _share of market_, he must first develop _share of mind_. In the long run, it is _share of mind_ which pulls the customer to the product. Although the customer may be drawn temporarily to a product because it is "new," "improved," "better than ever," or through a smart sales promotion, it is _share of mind_ advertising that creates product acceptance and loyalty.

As the product wins _share of mind_, its competitors lose it. If the concept presented to the customer is strong, appealing, and convincing, it may cause him to forget something he has already learned. Surveys indicate that it is possible to remove an advertising story from his mind and replace it with another. Then the ad man has won _share of mind_ and is on his way to winning _share of market_.

Contributions to Society Through Advertising

Critics find advertising a convenient symbol to express their general dissatisfaction with the American society and economy of today. But even the harshest critic will admit (reluctantly and with many qualifications) that advertising does, on occasion, serve the public well.

In the early years of this century, the California Fruit Growers Exchange (later the Sunkist Growers, Inc.) was in trouble. The supply of citrus fruit exceeded the demand, and trees had to be cut down to limit the crop. This waste of natural resources disturbed a Chicago advertising man. He got the account and introduced the American public to orange juice. Americans ate oranges, but very few had ever thought of drinking them. The idea caught on. The sale of oranges increased, and the trees were saved. An advertising campaign had revitalized an industry and introduced America to a new health habit.

The man who popularized orange juice was Albert D. Lasker, the father of modern advertising. Lasker knew that oranges contain Vitamin C, and he financed research which proved that Vitamin C is a vital element in diet. Lasker believed, and rightly so, that advertising had made a contribution to public health.[1]

Through the years, advertising has called on the consumer and introduced him to many products which have raised his standard of living and have made life more comfortable and pleasant for him. Household appliances, for example, can do the job better and faster than the housewife and, in addition, release her

[1] John Gunther, *Taken at the Flood* (New York: Harper, 1960), p. 72.

from the tedium of domestic chores and give her more time to pursue her interests.

What would happen if advertising were to stop?

Luther Hodges, who rose from farm boy to president of one of America's large corporations, then to Governor of North Carolina, and finally to Secretary of the Department of Commerce, has this to say:

> "Without advertising, our national per capita income would fall. The market demand for goods and services would shrink; production would fall off, and many jobs would disappear.

> "Without advertising, the consumer would in many instances pay more, not less, for consumer products.

> "Volume sales permit manufacturers to make profits on small margins per unit. If we were deprived of modern mass marketing, of which advertising is an essential ingredient, the prices of products would rise.

> "Without advertising, the consumer also would have to pay directly for the mass entertainment and the news and information services that are now financed largely out of advertising budgets." [1]

Advertising is only a part of the total selling picture. There are many other factors which contribute to successful selling. But if advertising *were* to stop, its loss would be felt by the American economy.

[1] Luther Hodges, "Advertising is Vital to Business," *Advertising Age* (January 15, 1963), p. 4.

Advertising has made contributions to our society by increasing interest in travel, music, books, art, fashion, and education. Public service campaigns have called attention to health and social problems, have furthered the cause of brotherhood and worship, and have won public support for charitable organizations.

Advertising is a tool for selling. Like any tool, its use depends on the man who is using it. It may be used with good or bad results. In the hands of the right man, the man who believes in advertising and understands its objectives, advertising can be memorable, imaginative, informative, and effective.

Personal Qualities

So what is he like, this right man for the advertising job? Study the career and personality of any successful ad man, and regardless of habits, convictions, characteristics (and in some cases, eccentricities), you are certain to find that he has these qualities:

He understands people. The layman often confuses understanding people with "getting along with people." These are not the same thing. The ad man has a product to sell, and to sell it he must learn all he can about his prospects. A good salesman always knows whom he is addressing, whether it is one person or thousands, even millions, of people. The ad man is sensitive to others – to their likes and dislikes, their needs and desires, their motivations. This sensitivity enables him to be right on target when he presents his message.

He has "know-how." Because he believes in advertising, in his agency, and in the products he represents, he is prepared to work hard. He realizes that he has as much opportunity as anyone else. He is considerate of other people and of their time. He cooperates with others when the cooperation of a group will get the job done best, or when others have procrastinated, he gets the job done himself. He understands the mechanics of the business. He takes the time to be sure; he doesn't work hurriedly or carelessly. He recognizes the importance of the job he is doing, no matter how small it may seem, for if the small jobs are done well, bigger jobs will come his way. He combines a capacity for hard work with a thorough knowledge of the business, with patience, with honesty, and with understanding and respect for others. He knows that success is not a gift bestowed indiscriminately, but a trophy for which he must compete.

He has initiative. Like a sense of humor, initiative is a popular quality which every man claims for himself, although he is quick to note the lack of it in others. In fact, initiative is a misunderstood characteristic. It doesn't mean simply seeing and doing the obvious on one's own. Initiative calls for a sort of x-ray vision, an ability to see beyond the obvious: it calls for extra thought, extra effort, and extra responsibility. A man with initiative is resourceful and inventive. He translates a thought into action, a dream into a reality. He recognizes a problem when he is exposed to it and takes steps to correct it. He anticipates a potential problem and takes steps to prevent it from occurring. He is the one who makes the first move; he is an originator. He is self-confident but not arrogant; he is active but not incautious. Initiative may mean the difference between being an outstanding salesman and an average salesman. And if this is true in selling, it is also true in advertising. It is especially true in account executive work.

He has intellectual curiosity. The man who has intellectual curiosity asks questions and seeks answers; he always wants to know more than he already knows; he uses his gift of intellect to learn and to understand. "Send me a man who reads!" says the International Paper Company advertisement. Yes, a man who reads, thinks, observes, reasons, and is continually in the process of expanding his horizons. Intellectual curiosity broadens his base. It gives him new exposure...new understanding...new ideas. And advertising is a business of producing new ideas.

No one has a copyright on ideas. Henry Ford's motor replaced the horse, but look at what has replaced the Model-T. A good idea never ends, because men with intellectual curiosity search for ways to make it even better.

It is characteristic of such men that they are able to challenge and stimulate others to develop intellectual curiosity. When presented with recommendations, men with intellectual curiosity respond with questions. "Why should we do it this way?" "What are your terms of reference?" "Is this right for us? Could it be made even better?"

A man who observes and studies what has been done in his own field, or in other fields, will find that his thinking has been sparked — an idea, an achievement may be adapted or expanded, improved upon or reconstructed into a new idea applicable to his own situation or problem. The idea may even be the starting point for a totally new concept.

One of the greatest benefits that an advertising agency man may offer his client is a new idea. And, because an advertising agency works in many different fields for many different clients, it is exposed to merchandising, selling, marketing, and advertising ideas in a broad spectrum of industries. Ideas may be borrowed in part from these different areas of exposure and constructed anew within other areas.

Intellectual curiosity is a quality of the advertising man who reads the trade and business papers looking for new and better ways of doing things and for ideas that may be adapted to his business or to his client's business.

Necessity, it has been said, is the mother of invention, but no one has ever named the father. What about intellectual curiosity? No invention, no idea, no discovery has ever been born that was not a result of intellectual curiosity.

He has self-discipline. Successful ad men, like successful salesmen, are made, not born. It is within the power of almost anyone to achieve success in the advertising profession if he will dedicate himself to the task. This requires a personal discipline, a discipline of one's self that is not easy to achieve. The demands a man makes on himself — *this is what I must do, this is what I must be* — are hard to fulfill when the man is his own teacher, his own master. It is all too easy to rationalize, to postpone, to make excuses, when the person to whom one is answering is oneself.

Self-discipline, self-control — call it what you will — starts when you set yourself a goal and commit yourself to achieving it. This personal commitment, coupled with a sighting of your course that never gets out of focus, makes failure all but impossible.

He has awareness. To be aware, the ad man must have met people at all levels. He would do well if he had clerked in a retail store, sold door-to-door, worked in a factory, and traveled extensively. He is well-read. His reading habits are well-balanced: they include news publications and publications edited to housewives or to any other single consumer or prospect group to whom the products he advertises are sold.

He displays good taste. In everything he does, he is setting a standard for his product, and if he is effective, he will influence the standards of the people to whom he is presenting his product. Good taste is important not only to effective selling, but also to the social responsibilities to which advertising must measure up. In the final analysis, the public will judge — like a jury at a trial — and the advertising man's work will be measured, not by a committee in an office, but by the customers in the market place.

CHAPTER SUMMARY

The Advertising Agency Man

He knows that advertising is a technique for selling, and that he is a salesman.

He knows that advertising's two primary objectives are *share of mind* and *share of market*.

He has these qualities:

> He understands people.
>
> He has "know-how."
>
> He has initiative.
>
> He has intellectual curiosity.
>
> He has self-discipline.
>
> He has awareness.
>
> He has good taste.

2
The
ad man
as a
marketing
researcher

The Ad Man as a Marketing Researcher

Ask a housewife to define marketing, and the chances are strong that she'll tell you it's going to the store to buy groceries. A businessman may think of marketing as getting a product to the market and selling it. In a sense, of course, both are right, since marketing is concerned with buying and selling. But there is a philosophy that lies behind successful marketing. A Marshall Field and Co. slogan says, "Give the lady what she wants," and this is part of the philosophy of marketing. Your product must be what the customer wants, or no sale. Before you can give the lady what she wants, however, you must *find out* what she wants. And to find out what she wants, you must *know her* — who she is, where she is, how she lives. You must see the product through her eyes in order to know if it is what she wants. *This, then, is the marketing concept: it is a philosophy of business in which the company sees its product through the eyes of the customer.*

Marketing recognizes the importance of defining the customers that a company wants to serve, of knowing all that can be learned about these customers, and using this knowledge in the conduct of business.

Once the customer has been identified, located, and his needs and desires determined, the company plans and organizes its activities to meet the customer's needs. The marketing-minded company knows its market; it knows its problem areas; it knows the obstacles it must overcome; it knows what opportunities have not yet been exploited. Using this knowledge, the company plans for each product or service.

How does the marketing-minded company acquire its customer-consciousness? How does it go about giving the lady what she wants?

The Marketing Concept

The marketing-minded company starts by understanding the seven component parts of the marketing concept, and by charting its course of action in relation to these components. They are:

1. **Market Research.** Market research is the means with which the company becomes acquainted with the customer. It answers these questions: Who is he? Where is he? How many of him are there? What does he need? What does he want? How may he satisfy his needs and wants?

2. **Product Research.** Product research develops new ideas for products, ways of improving existing products, or may eliminate products which have become ineffective or obsolete. In making product decisions, management utilizes information acquired through market research.

3. **Pricing.** Pricing is also based, in part, on information received from market research. Pricing answers these questions: What is the customer able to

pay? What are the company's costs and its profit objectives? What is the market and the competition?

4. Distribution Plans and Policy. How can the product most effectively be brought to the market? How may the customer be reached at the logical time to buy? How may all segments of distribution be coordinated effectively? This involves *strategy*.

5. Sales Objectives, Budgets, and Organization. Goals are set for salesmen and sales units. Expense is considered in relation to desired sales volume. What is the company's volume objective? What is the most profitable product mix? What are the percentages of the market objective in terms of customer types? The company must organize its sales department to take advantage of what market research has learned about the customer. In the light of this knowledge, how many salesmen should the company have, and where should they be located? How should they be trained, and what pay incentives are needed?

6. Advertising and Sales Promotion. This means communication with the customer, establishing in his mind a favorable attitude towards the product and motivating him to investigate buying it. It is selling and promoting on a broader basis, and more quickly than can be accomplished through personal contact.

7. Selling and Customer Service. Selling is person-to-person communication. All components of marketing should contribute to the effectiveness of selling. Customer service is a post-sales function of marketing which insures the customer's satisfaction and loyalty.

The marketing concept is crucial to the success of a company. Everything begins with the customer, who he is, where he is, what he is. A company which is not conscious of its customers is not communicating with them and is trying to deal with strangers about whom it knows little or nothing and whom, therefore, it cannot reasonably hope to satisfy. A company which does not embrace the marketing concept cannot be effective in its seven areas of planning and decision-making and will, as a coldly stated fact, lose business to its competitors.

Marketing Research

But how does the company meet and know its customers? Markets are widespread, and there can be no direct contact. And yet for the marketing concept to be translated into action, an almost personal knowledge of the customer is required. Between the customer and the company stand the middlemen — salesmen, retailers, jobbers — whose interpretations of the customer to the company and the company to the customer may vary widely. The answer is *marketing research*, an umbrella term which covers various types of research, which bridges the communications gap between the company and the customer.

Many large businesses have their own marketing research departments, and there are also firms which specialize in the field. But we are speaking here of the advertising man's role in marketing research.

In the advertising agency, marketing research helps to define advertising objectives, point out problems, and measure attitudes. It helps to define profitable markets; select the right media mix, the right packaging, pricing, merchandising, and sometimes the right form of the product itself. It should be emphasized here that marketing research lights the way, but does not make decisions. It *provides the information* for effective decision-making. The marketing expert can recommend decisions once the information is complete.

Types of Marketing Research

In the agency's responsibility, there are four types of marketing research which must be employed in developing the program. These are product research, market research, advertising research, and media research.

The ad man engaged in marketing research draws on his, and his client's, store of knowledge and experience. He refers back to work done successfully for other clients to give him reliable precedents. His research library gives him valuable information. His own good judgment plays an important role. And when there isn't enough information, he makes a formal study which involves testing in the field.

Now for a look at each of the four types of marketing research done by the agency.

Product Research. Product research means learning all there is to know about the product. And no less important, learning about the competitor's product. Both must be evaluated in the light of customer attitudes. Talks with consumers and retailers will reveal attitudes and show attributes the product must have to give it a competitive advantage. Research sets the potential for a product by checking its merits from the buyer's point of view. Research studies the package, the pricing, the brand name and the customer benefits. Having determined the product's strengths and weaknesses, the agency is in a position to suggest changes or improvements.

Market Research. Market research is concerned with locating and characterizing markets. Research will identify the user or potential user – his age, his income, his education, his residence, and what influences him to buy. What product does he buy now, is he satisfied or dissatisfied with it, and why?

The study of channels of distribution has become increasingly important as channels have become more widespread and various. Consider, for example, the number of items once sold only in drug stores which have now found new outlets in supermarkets and discount houses.

Advertising Research. Knowing the product, and knowing the market, it now becomes necessary to find the most effective way of telling the story of the product to the market. The ad, in whatever form it is presented, must be believable, informative, easy to understand, and memorable. Does it contain incentives which will move people to the product? What sounds and music will influence attitudes? Should the ad be in color or black and white? Is visual identification strong? If the ad is to be in print, each component part may be tested — the headline, the copy, the pictures, the situation. Often a panel of consumers will be asked to evaluate the product claims before it is given full-scale presentation. "After" tests may be made to measure the success of the ad in terms of recall, recognition, and sales results.

Media Research. Media research helps to determine the best way of reaching the defined market with the effective ad presentation. The richness of choice presents a complex problem — magazines, newspapers, billboards, radio, TV. Which of these media, or which combination of media, should be used for optimum results? Which magazines? How many colors should be used; what position or adjacency should be requested? How often should the ad be run? Or, what stations should be chosen, what programs, which days, what times? Audience analysis is aided by circulation audits and surveys which give insight into the selection of the right media.

How much advertising is the competition doing? An increased share of market cannot be obtained without increasing the share of total advertising dollars being spent in a given product category.

Marketing research studies, tests, and analyzes the product, the market, the message, and the medium. The end result of marketing research in the advertising agency's responsibility is the creation of more effective advertising and the spending of the money in the wisest possible way.

CHAPTER SUMMARY

The Ad Man as a Marketing Researcher

He understands the marketing concept – the philosophy of business that sees the product through the eyes of the customer.

He uses marketing research to provide information for decision-making in these areas:

> to define advertising objectives
>
> to point out problems
>
> to measure attitudes
>
> to define profitable markets
>
> to select the right media mix, packaging, pricing, merchandising, and, frequently, the form of the product itself.

In the advertising agency responsibility, there are four types of marketing research:

> *product research* – learning all there is to know about the product and the competitor's product.
>
> *market research* – locating and characterizing markets.
>
> *advertising research* – finding the most effective way of telling the story of the product to the market.
>
> *media research* – determining the best way of reaching the market with the ad presentation.

3
The
ad man
as an
account
executive

The Ad Man as an Account Executive

Account executives, in books and dramas, are seldom called upon to do anything but save the account (even at the risk of losing their own souls in the process). Their real-life counterparts, however, have many areas of responsibility and may be called upon to play many different roles: administrator, writer, editor, salesman, merchandiser, marketer, diplomat, friend, guide, and counselor.

The ad man who is an account executive knows what the ad business is all about. *It is making better ads and attending to the needs of the clients.* As an account executive, he oversees both. He maintains contact with the client, interpreting the agency to him. He also interprets the client to the agency. He supervises the execution of work done for the client. He is responsible for the preparation and placing of advertising. He is sent as an emissary to win new clients. And he is a friend and advisor to existing clients. At times, he may feel like the parent of a large family who must convince his brood that he loves each of them equally. And this is true – he does, because his agency has integrity, and so does he. He doesn't advertise products which he doesn't believe in. A small account, a large account, an old account, a new account – he sees to it that each one receives a fair measure of his, and his agency's, time and talents.

Time is a key word. There are deadlines to be met. There are decisions to be made. There are problems to be solved. There is thinking to be done – a great campaign is usually not the result of a brain wave, but of brain work. The often quoted Parkinson's First Law states: "Work expands to meet the time available." This is illustrated by the case of the little old lady with nothing but time on her hands who managed to make an entire day's project of writing, stamping, addressing, and mailing a post card to her nephew. In the ad man's case, the law should be reversed: time expands to meet the work that must be done. He is the type of man who not only works efficiently under a heavy work load, but who also actually thrives under pressure. To expand time to meet his work load, the ad man must be able to *organize,* for there are only a given number of hours in each day.

The First Ability: To Organize Your Work

Some people have a hard time getting organized, and this is certain to be an obstacle to success in any career. The man who fails to develop the ability to organize runs hard and gets nowhere, like a squirrel on a treadmill. When selecting a man for account executive duties, look first at his ability to organize.

A management consultant called on an industrialist and told him that he could show him the way to increase the efficiency of his operation within three months. The industrialist was a busy man with many problems, and he said he couldn't take the time to listen to a lot of high-flown, theoretical, nonsense. "I can tell you in three minutes," said the consultant. "Furthermore, I'll bet you $50,000 that my way works. If I'm wrong, all you have to lose is three minutes of your time. If I'm right, you'll lose $50,000, but you'll find it was worth every cent of it when you see the effect on your business." The industrialist was skeptical but curious, and he took the bet. The consultant handed him a sheet of paper. "Make a list of everything you need to do within the next three months in order of importance. Then start with the first item and work your way down the list. If you're interrupted, be sure to start again where you left off." Three months later, the consultant had his $50,000. And the industrialist was a happy loser for, as the consultant had predicted, the simple idea had actually benefited his business.

The account executive, like the industrialist, will find that making and following a plan of action increases his efficiency, clarifies his thinking, and saves him time, effort, and frustration. Plan, organize, put first things first, follow through on the work plan. A navigator wouldn't start on a voyage without charts, an architect has his blueprint — but how many people in business actually map out a course of action for themselves? The good account executive does. As a result, he can see where he has been and where he is going. He helps himself, his agency, and his clients when he organizes his work, completing his job objectives in order of priority.

The Second Ability: To Plan The Marketing Strategy

The proliferation of products on today's market is remarkable, and the resulting competition for share of mind and share of market is intense. The consumer's mind is constantly being bombarded by an ever-increasing number of advertising messages.

But the consumer's mind has a good defense against this massive and continual bombardment. It has a natural resistance that makes it virtually impregnable to any message that doesn't relate in some way to knowledge or experience that the mind has already assimilated. An example of this rejection at work: Research has shown that a large percentage of television viewers frequently misidentify the product advertised, attributing the commercial to *the product leader in the field.*

All this underlines the fact that in the battle for share of mind and share of market, strategy is a prerequisite for victory. Creativity is a powerful weapon — but first there must be a battle plan. And it is the account executive, primarily, who has the responsibility for formalizing the marketing strategy.

The plan must set out where the product is to be sold, how it is to be sold, the market to whom it has the strongest appeal, and how it is to be priced. In the plan he must clearly define what the consumer thinks about the product, what he would *like* the consumer to think about it, and how much money it will take to reach the marketing objectives. As strategist, the account executive is committed to objectivity. Information comes not off the top of his head but from the marketplace. He must take a broad view of the product field. It is a tactical error to focus almost exclusively on the merits and demerits of the individual product, giving the competition only token attention.

The Importance of Positioning

In fact, it might be said that "Don't ignore the enemy," is the keystone of the positionists' philosophy. Positioning is an advertising creed of the 70's which gives new, fresh emphasis to the importance of strategy. The average consumer, positionists point out, is exposed to more than half a million advertising messages in a year. In such a fiercely competitive time, image advertising in itself is not enough (*everyone* is doing it). To win in today's market, you must relate your product to the competition.

This does not mean hand-to-hand combat in which you directly attack the leader in a given product field with the hope of dislodging it from its position of pre-eminence. There are too many examples of this misdirected strategy. Perhaps the most ironic example occurred when Xerox went into computer territory and IBM invaded copier country, and both bombed. In the consumer's mind, Xerox is the giant in the copier field, IBM is the giant in the computer field, and never the twain shall meet. These positions are firmly established in the consumer's mind, and yet he was being asked to think "Xerox means computers and IBM means copiers." No way. This was a major strategical error.

Strategy in today's market employs psychological warfare. The account executive considers and compares his product and competitive products and then recommends how the product should be positioned in relation to the competition. He doesn't try to displace or replace the competition. Instead, he finds an unoccupied place for his product that locates it in the product field – and in the consumer's mind. By relating his product to information about the competition that is already stored in the consumer's mind, he gets the consumer to accept messages about his product instead of rejecting them.

Avis is a clear-cut and classic example of effective positioning. "We're Number 2," said Avis, thus relating itself to the leader in the field (and also to the lesser competition). The rest is history. Avis entered the consumer's mind and established itself as the lovable underdog, always trying harder, and succeeded in winning share of mind and share of market. Then there was 7-Up. 7-Up staked out a place for itself in the country of the mind by relating to the giant, Coca-Cola, but in a negative way: "7-Up, the Un–Cola," the *alternative* to Coke.

"We're Number 2." "The Un–Cola." "Think Small." "The Friendly Skies." "It's the Real Thing." Great slogans because they are the creative expression of carefully thought-out marketing strategy.

Successful marketing strategy must also involve long-range thinking and planning. Change pervades our lives as traditions are broken and the social structure is reshaped. When the battle plan is set, it must not be vulnerable to change for the sake of change, or change will defeat it. If one plans not for the year ahead, but for the years ahead, change can be an ally rather than an enemy, offering new opportunities for growth.

Of late, creativity buffs have been critical of the strategists (positionists in particular), accusing them of relegating creativity to the attic, an obsolete relic of the past that has outlived its usefulness and now has only a historical interest pleasantly tinged with nostalgia.

Looking at it practically, the truth is that "creativity" and "positioning" are simply new names for processes that are as old as advertising itself. One is not necessarily more important than the other. A masterful strategy will fail unless it is carried out creatively. And so will the most creative advertising campaign unless it springs from a sound strategy and correct positioning of the product.

Each successful campaign must begin with marketing strategy; this is why the ability to counsel in the development of a winning strategy is a "must" for the account executive.

The Third Ability: To Produce Ideas

An account executive must have the ability to produce ideas. The very thought of having to produce ideas constantly awes many. "You have to be a genius," they say. "It's a gift."

The ability to produce ideas is not necessarily a gift, nor is its possession limited to the genius. An account executive who consciously sets out to train himself can make idea-producing a habit. How? Try this. Look at everything with a speculative eye. When you see an article of merchandise, ask yourself if it could be made better, packaged better, or advertised and sold in a better way. *Punctuate your thinking with question marks, not with periods.* Look around you every day with fresh eyes — in your home, in your office, in your world. Look long and hard at familiar objects. Think about what you would do to make them better. Some of your first ideas for improvement may seem foolish, but what you are doing is training your eyes to see with new understanding.

The idea-producing ability, then, stems from a way of thinking which combines constant exercise of the imagination with a questioning eye and a roving curiosity. A mind grooved in this pattern will respond to problems by generating ideas almost instinctively.

Why should the account executive be called upon to generate ideas? Because he is in the business of producing and selling ideas. It's his job. And it is important to keep in mind that big ideas in advertising are not limited to copy ideas. The account executive will be called upon to produce ideas in every area of agency responsibility. A product improvement idea, a merchandising idea, a sales incentive idea, a packaging idea – any idea in any area, no matter how modest it may seem at the time of its inception, may prove to be a big idea in terms of results produced.

Sometimes techniques are mistaken for ideas. A technique is not really an idea; it is simply a way of presenting an idea. If the idea is not sound, the technique means nothing. A campaign may fail because a technique has been mistaken for an idea.

A good idea, poorly presented, is still a good idea.

A bad idea, well presented, is still a bad idea.

A good idea, well presented, is a great idea. The technique of presentation can call attention to the good idea, complement it and enhance it.

The Fourth Ability: To Make an Effective Presentation

An account executive must have the ability to communicate effectively. He must sell the ideas that he and others in the agency produce. His written presentation to the client (and his oral one) must be vigorous and forceful.

Writing the plan for a client's advertising program is critically important. Ideas formalized in writing give the client a tangible instrument he can use in decision-making. It is in the plan that the account executive, through suggestion or implication, gives the client his reason to buy the agency's recommendations. It is the plan that explains clearly and logically how the advertising program has been organized. The plan also sets a timetable for action.

There is no "standard form" for written presentations. However, all of them contain essentially the same ingredients. The first section defines the product, the market, and the objectives of the program. It summarizes criteria applicable to the budget, the product, and the advertising message (both the copy and the design approach).

The next section gives an analysis of media and presents recommendations, with the cost efficiencies for each. Next, the outline of scheduling within each media category tells when the advertising will appear, where it will appear, and how it will be merchandised. The final item is a summation of costs (both time or space and production) for each medium.

Most important, each presentation should zero in on the needs and goals of the advertiser and should have a clear point of emphasis. Market research, creative concept, sales promotion and the like should be oriented to solving the most pressing problem of the moment.

It is the account executive who assembles the information and prepares the presentation; this is one of his major responsibilities.

In summary, the account executive organizes his work and time; he determines strategy; he generates ideas; he presents the program. These abilities are so important that the lack of any one of them will be a definite and obvious handicap. But a handicap may be overcome by patience, perseverance, self-discipline, and the will to win.

Responsibilities

Let's look now at the account executive's responsibilities in planning, organizing, and carrying out an advertising campaign. There are ten steps to be taken.

1. **He defines the product.** This involves preparing a fact sheet. What is the product? How is it used? What features does it have? Who are the major competitors? How does the product differ from its competitors'? What are its advantages? Disadvantages?

2. **He defines the market.** Who are the product's buyers or potential buyers? Where are they? How large is the market? What are its demographic and geographic characteristics? Where is the 20% that buys 80%? (This is generally true of most companies.) What are the channels of distribution? How does the product get to market?

3. **He positions the product.** Where is the opportunity, and what strategy should be employed? What *share of mind* can be achieved — and at what cost?

4. **He defines the objective of the campaign** in relation to the problem. What *share of mind* does the product currently have, and what *share of market*? What are the specific goals for this particular campaign? What is advertising's responsibility to be in the company's total marketing plan? Is it to produce inquiries for the sales department? To create a favorable climate for salesmen's personal calls? To introduce customers to a new product? To emphasize new features of an existing product? To improve the image of the company or product? To overcome buyer objections? Defining the advertising goal will almost always involve solving a specific problem. The problem

must be recognized and stated correctly in order to find the right solution, the objective of the campaign.

5. He is an important member of the agency creative team that will decide on the creative concept. The product, the market, the distribution, and the advertising objective have been defined, so that what to say is well documented. The problem is how to say it.

6. He will determine how much money is needed and how to spend it, with the assistance and counsel of his account supervisor (a senior account executive whose experience qualifies him to oversee the work done on the account and to pass judgment on decisions). This involves *writing the media plan*. The media plan will commit the money to the media which will most effectively reach the market and influence it. Here the account executive will ask for recommendations from the media department because the media selected will influence the form of the ad presentation. If the estimated budget exceeds the amount that the client is prepared to spend, it will be necessary for the account executive to go back to the client to change his thinking (or to have the client change the agency's thinking). If the product is under-advertised, the rewards of the campaign are not likely to meet the objectives set — there is no profit in under-advertising.

7. He sets up budgets and schedules.

8. The ads are written and prepared. The degree of his involvement will depend on his talents and experience. If he has come through copy or art, he can contribute effectively. If not, he must depend on the talents of others.

9. **He plans the merchandising.** This is to engage enthusiastic support from salesmen, distributors, and retailers for the advertising program before the advertising appears.

10. **He manages the money.** This is his overall responsibility throughout the campaign. His agency must earn a good profit, the advertiser must receive a good value, and the money must be allocated and spent in a way to get good results.

CHAPTER SUMMARY

The Ad Man as an Account Executive

He knows what the ad business is all about; it is making better ads and attending to the needs of the client. He oversees both.

He interprets the client to the agency, the agency to the client.

He has the ability to:

1. Organize his work.
2. Plan the marketing strategy.
3. Produce ideas.
4. Make an effective presentation.

He plans and supervises the work that is done for the client:

1. He defines the product.
2. He defines the market.
3. He positions the product.
4. He defines the advertising goal.
5. He is an important member of the agency team that will decide on the creative concept.
6. Advised and assisted by his account supervisor, he determines how much money is needed and how to spend it.
7. He sets up budgets and schedules.
8. The ads are written and prepared. His degree of involvement depends on his talents and experience.

9. He plans the merchandising.
10. He manages the money.

4
The
ad man
as a
salesman

The Ad Man as a Salesman

In attending to the needs of his clients, the account executive must, if he is to be effective, be a good salesman. Why? Because it is his job to sell ideas. In the ad business, the most brilliant, creative idea will never see the light of day unless someone buys it. And management cannot be expected to recognize a good idea unless it is presented by a good salesman.

Elmer Wheeler built a large and successful sales training school on the theory that salesmen are not born, they are made. All of us have known men who prove his theory true. The chronicles of American business are full of examples of shy, introverted people who have become successful salesmen. There are certain prerequisites — good manners, product knowledge — but the secret of success in selling is in learning how to get in step with other people.

Too many men who consider themselves good salesmen are, in truth, not. These are the men who look upon the sales territory as a general might look upon a battlefield. To such a salesman, the businessman is his opponent. The businessman has the money, and the salesman's objective is to conquer him and bring the money back to his own troops. Unfortunately, there are sales managers who expound this philosophy.

Buyer-Seller Relationship

The good salesman has to have the client's best interests foremost in his mind. To do this, the salesman must understand the client's problem or objective. Recommendations as to what he should buy or how the money should be spent should only be made on the basis of how the problem can be most effectively solved or the objective met. To do otherwise is to invite doubt as to competence.

In the advertising agency business, you enjoy a continuing relationship with your clients. Confidence grows as problems are solved and objectives are reached. No one, however, is always right. In addition, the forces at work in the market place are constantly changing. For this reason, you must have the ability to act and react quickly. When a mistake is made, admit it. Stop the money and get back on the track as fast as possible.

In the buyer-seller relationship, there are several basics to keep in mind.

1. People prefer to feel that they have bought something, rather than that they have been sold something.

2. It is easier and less risky for the buyer to make a series of small decisions, rather than one big decision.

3. Many a successful businessman would rather see his idea put into effect than your idea. (With some

people, this is true 100% of the
time.)

In the agency business, as in any other business,
you will need new business in order to grow and to
provide increased opportunity for employees. You
cannot stand still, or soon others will pass by you.
Furthermore, you will lose some business; this loss will
have to be replaced with new business.

Losing Clients: Reasons

Business losses will occur for a variety of
reasons.

1. You may have failed to attend
   sufficiently to your client's needs.
2. You may have failed to produce
   better advertising at a given
   moment for a specific client.
3. You may have failed to manage
   the budget efficiently, including
   production costs and media
   purchases.
4. Personnel changes within the
   client's organization can be a
   reason. New management may have
   a closer relationship with, or a
   preference for, another agency.
5. You may lose an account executive
   in your organization and the client
   may follow him to another agency.

---

6. Company mergers, product
   obsolescence or market down-turns
   within industries may also cost you
   clients or a severe reduction in
   their advertising programs, from
   time to time.

Program Expansion for Current Clients

To replace this loss of business and to win the
additional business essential to agency growth, you can
look in two directions – to the expansion of existing
clients' programs and to new clients.

Look first to your current clients. They deserve
top priority. Frequently, they are not doing as much
as they should be doing or would like to be doing,
because of overworked top management (and lack of
time to initiate), or because you have not been doing
all your homework and have not sold them on the
value of expanding their activity in specific directions.

The *selling of a new idea* to a client is an almost
impossible task on the first approach. For this reason,
you should consider using two calls: the first a
"staging call," the second a "selling call." The staging
call is made after you have "thought out" the problem
and "thought in" the solution. The purpose of the
staging call is to review the problem with the client
and to discuss possible solutions. Among the solutions
discussed is the one that you believe to be right. It is
very easy to direct special emphasis to your idea in
the conversation. Most likely the client will add to it

certain refinements and suggestions out of his wisdom, experience, and product knowledge. This is good and desirable. It is often possible to make the idea *his* idea, or at least a combination of his idea and your idea. Remember, it is his money, not yours. It is his company, not yours. The more the idea becomes his, the greater the possibility that it will become an outstanding success. Seldom is advertising an isolated factor in a company's marketing mix. The involvement of people at the company level early in the conceptual stage is important. If it is not forthcoming, you had better look for another idea.

A word of caution here. Please do not construe the above to mean that you should be a "yes" man. Just the opposite. If the client has an idea of merit, consider it. If it is good after thoroughly thinking it out, use it. If parts of his idea are good and parts are not, keep only the good parts. It is your responsibility to come up with the program. But once you have done so, it is equally important that it becomes the client's program, not just yours.

Winning New Clients

In most agencies, the account executive will share some of the new business (new clients) development activity. Winning new clients is an exciting and rewarding experience. There is no one formula, but there are certain helpful guidelines which you can follow to make the use of your time more productive.

1. Think in terms of either product
   categories or geographical areas.
   You will be seeking a new client in
   a specific product field (because
   you feel competent and are
   interested) or in a certain city or
   area (because you can efficiently
   service his account).

2. Know your agency story and
   philosophy thoroughly. If you are
   using the "product category"
   approach, do your homework so
   you know as much as possible
   about his industry. If you are using
   the "geographical area" approach,
   know all you can about the various
   industries of your current clients.
   Be up to date on current national
   and international business trends.

3. When you make a new business
   call, you will talk about two things.
   His business. Your business. Be
   prepared to apply the philosophy
   of your business to his business on
   the spot.

4. Keep your sales approach flexible.
   Remember, prospects are people,
   individuals who are different.

5. It is important to be as good a
   listener. Only by getting the
   prospect to tell you about his

company and his problems will you
have the opportunity to apply the
value of your agency's service to
his business.

Talking About a Prospect's Company

How do you get the prospect to tell you about
his company? You ask him questions. You do exactly
the same thing Dale Carnegie tells you to do in "How
to Win Friends and Influence People." You listen
while the prospect talks about his interests. Maybe, for
an "ice-breaker," you talk about his family (is there a
photo on his desk?) or deep-sea fishing (is there a
sailfish on the wall?) or hunting. Look for clues about
his office or get one from his secretary before you go
in. Shortly, you shift the conversation to his other big
interest...his business.

In getting him to talk about his business, keep in
mind that you will have to know certain things before
you can successfully apply the benefits of your agency
service to his advertising, sales, or marketing needs. A
very high percentage of all agency new business sales
are made on the first call (even though the contract
may be signed later).

If he jumps the gun and asks you what you can
do for him, answer him this way. "It would be very
difficult to give you meaningful recommendations
without some background from you on your current
situation. I'm sure you have some objectives that are
not being reached. Every business does. Which come
to your mind immediately?"

If he responds, the ice is broken. Follow his line of conversation, leading to his biggest problem and why it is. If he does not respond specifically, go to the distribution question.

"Could we take a quick look at your distribution?"

Even if the prospect does not ask you for recommendations (and in most cases he will not), lead with the distribution question, "How and where is your product distributed?" Use a blank map as a visual aid. Hand him your pen and let him mark on it. This map will prove a handy reference for you after the interview is over. Also, it will give you an insight into his channels of distribution and into some of his problems.

Talking About Your Agency

The ideal way to tell the agency story is to integrate it with the prospect's story. Explain your agency service in helping solve problems as it relates to his problems. *Do not get into your story until it relates.* The failure to follow this rule is possibly the most frequent mistake made by most men in new business solicitation.

Specific Questions to Ask

Succeeding questions in order are:

"Where are your wholesale outlets? Which does the best job? The worst? What is their margin?"

"How many retailers? Is your market coverage balanced? Have you considered other types of retail stores? What margin do they earn? Volume discounts? Sales incentives? How do your distributors and retailers rate your brand in comparison to the competitions' brands? Who are your leading competitors? How do they rate in comparison with your brand? What was the situation three years ago? Five? Ten? What share of market does each have? What share do you have? What would you like to have?"

"What features **does** your product have that your competitors' products lack? How is your product different? Are any changes contemplated? How soon? What is your main selling feature?"

"How many employees do you have?" Or, "What is your annual volume?" (The answer to either question will give you an index as to his potential ad budget. There is a definite ratio of employees to gross sales for every industry, just as there is an average percentage of sales spent for advertising for each industry. See the "Useful Information Section" at the back of the book.)

"How many salesmen do you employ? How are they compensated? Can they do more? What is their biggest problem?"

"What, in your opinion, is your biggest sales problem?"

How to Close

By this point in the interview, you should have earned the confidence of the prospect. You have a reasonable understanding of his market, his product, and his most critical problem. He understands how you have helped other companies solve similar problems.

It's time to close. This is done by *focusing on his biggest problem* (it may even be the one that you have suggested). If you really know your business you can suggest a solution right then.

In nearly all cases, your sale will be made by conceiving and presenting a *big idea* solution to the prospect's most pressing problem. The big idea may be a marketing concept, a merchandising or sales promotion plan, a packaging innovation, a unique media use, a selling strategem, or a fresh creative approach. Few, if any, visuals are needed as a rule. The *idea* in answer to the problem is the key. To bring it off and make the sale, the psychology of selling is all-important. If you want to be a successful new-business salesman, you will do well to study the psychology of selling.

If the prospect finds merit in your big idea, *suggest a timetable for putting it into effect.* Do not ask him for his account. Ask him to let you help him to improve his problem situation. His agreement will automatically land you the account, if you carry out your end of the bargain. (Recall point 2 in the buyer-seller relationship at the start of this chapter. "It is much easier and less risky for the buyer to make a series of small decisions than one big one.")

Important Considerations

If the prospect should ask you to formalize your idea on paper so that he can review it with his associates, agree to do so. Give the prospect and yourself a definite timetable to work against. Set the date for the next meeting as soon as possible. Fires that are not refueled quickly turn to embers, then to ashes.

If he should ask you to do any extended market research, art work or other creative work, ask him for a budget. Have an understanding that if the material submitted is accepted, the cost will be included in your normal agency charge or commission. If it is not accepted, the material is his upon payment of the agreed-upon budget figure.

Never spend money on a speculative presentation. If the prospect is to seriously consider a new program, it is important that he have a financial interest in it. Otherwise, his interest will be something less than primary. Only go so far as to document your ideas with examples of what you have done for other clients. There is only one exception. That is when the head of the business has definitely assured you that he will give you his account if you can demonstrate your ability to improve his advertising program.

In soliciting an account, it is usually best to call first on the president of the company. Sooner or later, he is the man who will decide to appoint the agency or to approve the decision. Initially, the president will either hear you out or will suggest that you talk first with the marketing manager, the sales manager, the public relations director, or the advertising manager. In turn, this person will normally go back to the president for his approval before any decision is made.

When the account is yours, don't stop selling. The service that you render to a client after winning the account is a continuation of the selling process. "After" is as important as "before," for the key to really good selling is *service.*

CHAPTER SUMMARY

The Ad Man as a Salesman

He is a good listener — he lets the prospect do most of the talking.

He isolates the prospect's problems — and relates the problems to his agency's experience in solving similar problems.

He finds out the prospect's biggest problem — and offers a solution in terms of a big idea.

He sets a timetable for himself and his prospective client to work against.

After the account is his, he continues to sell by giving good service to the client.

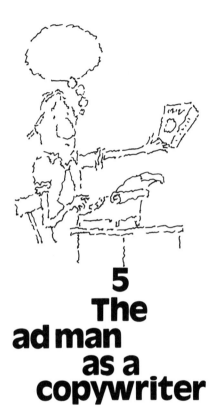

5
The
ad man
as a
copywriter

The Ad Man as a Copywriter

The copywriter has a responsibility to advertising as a business, and to all those whose jobs and lives depend on the successful sale of the products he is advertising. But occasionally there is one who does not recognize this truth. He is a free spirit. He knows his market through intuition; he gets his big ideas through inspiration; and he turns them into creative copy through the use of his imagination.

At least that is the thesis of copywriter Hugo McOstrich who, in the following interview reprinted with the permission of *Obscure* magazine, lets the reader in on...

How to Write Ineffective Advertising Copy

"Hugo, in the year that you've been in advertising, you've made quite a name for yourself. How about letting the readers of *Obscure* in on some of your secrets? Tell us how you go about creating ineffective ads."

"I'll be happy to. I noticed you used the word 'creating.' That's it, baby, the whole shooting match. Creativity. You've got to have it. It's a gift, man."

"Yes, I'm sure it is."

"You gotta make ads that are different, original, like nothing no one's ever seen before. And that takes creativity. That's it, that's the whole shooting —"

"Ah, yes, I'm sure it is, you're right, Hugo. Now let me ask you about research."

"About *what*?"

"Research. Don't you do a certain amount of research before writing the ad? Familiarizing yourself with the product and the market?"

"That's stifling, man. Research is for plodders. When you've got imagination and brains, who needs facts? Me, I sit down and create, get right to it. No point wasting time doing research. Copywriting is a 20th century art form; it's self-expression. There are a lot of people who don't realize that."

"I have to confess, I'm one of them. Isn't the basic purpose of the ad to sell the product?"

"Oh, sure, sure. Thing is, you gotta be clever. Way out. You need impact. POW!"

"I see. Now, Hugo, what about the market, the people you're writing to? How do you determine what will appeal to them? Don't you have to know how they live, what their needs are, and so on?"

"I hate people. Never go near 'em, if I can help it. I'm kind of a loner. Like my ivory tower, you know?"

"You rely on surveys, then? Or reading some of the same publications your prospects read?"

"Watch it. You're accusing me of doing research again."

"Sorry. I suppose you do check on competitors' products and study their current campaigns?"

"You haven't got the picture yet. I create, I don't copy. It all comes out of my head. The less I know about competitors' products, the better I like it."

"What you're saying is that you start writing the ad with an empty mind?"

"Let's not say empty, let's say *open*. My mind's not cluttered with facts, it's receptive to these flashes of inspiration..."

"Tell me this, Hugo, does it help you to outline the objectives of the ad campaign before you begin to write?"

"No, no, no! No tedious paper work. It comes to me as I write."

"How many versions of an ad will you do before you're satisfied?"

"What do you mean?"

"Don't you try several different copy approaches, play around with ideas?"

"No, I write the ad, and that's it. I don't want to lose my wonderful wit and spontaneity — it comes right off the top of my head, you know? And I don't ever rewrite. I think you lose something rewriting."

"The wonderful wit and spontaneity?"

"That's right. I don't let other guys play around with my ads, either. Their advice is not welcome, and if they give it anyway, I ignore it. No one's going to whittle down *my* talent."

"Hugo, here's something all our readers will want to know. What, in your opinion, is the most ineffective ad you've ever written?"

"Sweetie, that's a real toughie; there've been so many in my meteoric career. I guess my masterpiece was the one I did for Glacier Refrigerator. I had this blonde babe in a bikini, see, sitting cross-legged on top of a Glacier fridge, and my headline was COOL IT. No brand name. The picture told the story. That was it. It was smashing."

"I know it was, Hugo, I saw it. How did you follow it up?"

"I was going to have this couple dressed out as Eskimos, see, buying a fridge, and my headline was PEOPLE IN THE KNOW, KNOW. But it didn't come off."

"No?"

"No, the Glacier people cancelled."

"Hugo, I certainly want to thank you for giving us this interview. Just one more question. What are you working on currently?"

"I'm not."

"You're not working on a campaign?"

"I'm not working."

"You're no longer with John, Wellington, and Boots?"

"Let's just say I outgrew the agency. There wasn't enough room there to contain my genius. And the boys at the office apparently never heard that we're supposed to be living in the sweet land of liberty."

"Oh?"

"They didn't believe in freedom of expression. It was *stifling* there. I could feel the creative juices drying up."

"Hugo, I'm sure the readers of *Obscure* will agree with me when I say that you really have earned your reputation as a master of ineffective advertising. Thank you so much, and lots of luck."

If you think that Hugo McOstrich exists only in someone's nightmare, open any magazine or newspaper and glance through it. You won't have any trouble picking out the McOstrich ads. These writers have never learned, or they have forgotten, that *advertising is selling.* If they made a personal presentation in the manner in which their ads were presented, they would be laughed out of the room.

You might call these ads "Protest" ads, because their creators are insisting on the "right" to "freedom of expression" which, they claim, is a necessary adjunct to "creativity." They ignore the fact that

freedom is *not* the right to do as one wishes. Freedom
is the right to think clearly and to make one's own
decisions and choices instead of being arbitrarily
controlled by another person or power. But, these
decisions are made within the framework of moral,
social, and political laws. Pure "freedom," involving no
recognition of principles and ethics, is irresponsible
and can only lead to disorder, violence, and anarchy.
The word "freedom" is meaningless if there are no
standards of behavior upon which to base one's
decisions.

On a smaller scale, each profession and business
has its own standards. The ad makers who blatantly
ignore the disciplines of their profession are abusing
their freedom, not using it. But they will defend their
work. It's "different." "Unique." "Witty." "Artistic."
Most of the ads, however, are ads for their creators'
talents. What they sell is not the product, but the
presentation.

There are others, of course, who make
ineffective ads. The Backslapper is loud and hearty, a
braggart. He talks big, tries to bully the prospect into
buying the product. Superlatives are his specialty. No
need for sticking to the facts. If he tells you his
product is THE GREATEST, it is. His enthusiasm is
contagious – like a bad cold. No one will come near
him.

His opposite number is the Shrinking Violet.
Modest and introverted, he hides under his hat and
limits himself to a dry recitation of the facts. He's
kind of shy. Scared of lively verbs. He certainly

wouldn't want to *force* his product's charms on anyone, and he doesn't. His ads go unnoticed.

The Clown's copy is more fun than a barrel of monkeys. Watch him juggle those adjectives; he's going to keep a dozen going at once. Tasty, tempting, tantalizing, zestful, refreshing, invigorating – whoops! Oh, well, better luck next time.

The Great American Novelist hasn't written the Great American Novel yet, but he's getting good experience writing copy – gives him the opportunity to develop his style. So you're not quite sure what he's selling? You can at least admire the way he turns a phrase; who knows, he may be the one to fill Hemingway's shoes.

Then there's the Egghead. A man of many words, all of them long ones. Words of three, four, five, or more syllables. Compound words. Long complex sentences. He's the one who calls a spade "an excavating implement." When you read his ads, keep a dictionary at your elbow. You'll need it.

Finally, there's the Thrifty Scotsman who is out to lower costs by doing several advertising jobs in one ad. It's a black day for him when he can't get at least a dozen sales points into his copy. His illustration and his headline never say the same thing. You've got to admire the way he packs an ad with sales points, even though you can't remember one of them after you've read the ad.

Ads by the assortment of ad makers just catalogued are dull or confusing or even offensive. The sales messages they present are obscured by the style of presentation. They may lack the bravura and showmanship of McOstrich ads, but they are equally ineffective.

But that's enough of horrible examples. Let's look now at the other side of the coin, effective advertising, and see how it is created.

How to Write Effective Advertising Copy

You, the copywriter, may be said to be playing the role of matchmaker, for you are trying to bring the prospect and the product together. But you can't count on love at first sight. Others are courting your prospect, too. The average person, we are told, has a potential exposure to some 2800 commercial messages a week. The competition is stiff. How are you to attract the prospect's attention to your product, win his approval of it, and make him remember it favorably?

Remember those comic strips in which an electric light bulb flashed on over a character's head when he'd had a brilliant idea? Most laymen tend to think that this is how copywriters operate, that they are suddenly "seized" by an illuminating idea, and a great ad is born then and there with no preceding gestation period. It is true that an effective copywriter may be doing some such homely thing as singing in the shower when he is suddenly inspired; the answer comes into his head — the way to make the public love his product. *But* he has worked long and hard to reach this stage of the creative process.

How long does it take to create a great advertising program? Charles Adams of McManus, John, and Adams, in his book, *Common Sense In Advertising*, says, "Sometimes you can do it in ten minutes – after ten hours of thinking; after ten years of practice."[1] (And after weeks, or even months, of time-consuming but all-important copy research.) Adams divides the time required to produce a great ad campaign into three stages. First, he says, there is a *period of ingestion*. This is when the fact-finding is done, when the objectives are set, the competition studied, the product and the market analyzed. Then there is a *period of incubation*. This is a period of assimilation, when you absorb everything you have learned in the first stage. And finally comes *inspiration*.[2] It will come only after the first two stages have been passed.

Ingestion, incubation, inspiration – three steps in the creative process. This brings us, inevitably, to that word "creativity," which is probably the most overworked word in advertising's lexicon. Lately the word has entered the public domain and has come to be synonymous with the works of the new, young agencies. Creativity, however, was born before Mary Wells. The history of advertising is studded with great campaigns, creative campaigns. And any copywriter would do well to study them. Not to imitate, but to learn basic principles and techniques. The works of the masters can show us what makes advertising work.

[1] Charles Adams, *Common Sense In Advertising* (New York: McGraw-Hill, 1965), p. 142.
[2] Ibid. pp. 142, 143.

To "create" means to have the ability to cause something new to come into existence. Creativity in advertising, then, might be said to mean to have the ability to invent an "effective" ad campaign. If it isn't effective, that is, if it fails to accomplish the campaign objective, it is not creative.

Stating the Problem and Formulating the Objective

The creative process doesn't begin until the problem has been properly defined and the copy approach decided upon. It is not always an easy task to define the problem. The problem is not a symptom, but the disease itself. Many diseases may cause a high fever; the proper treatment can't be given until the specific disease is identified. In the same way, declining share of market is a symptom that something is wrong, and the problem must be defined before the situation may be corrected.

Once the problem has been correctly defined, an advertising objective may be formulated. This gives the campaign planners a positive direction to follow. They know what they want the campaign to accomplish, what part it should play in solving the problem.

The degree of product acceptance and product difference must be considered during the planning, for this will determine the amount of total sell or how much of the story to tell.

If the product is in the *pioneering stage* — that is, if it is a new and different product which has never been on the market before — it will probably be necessary to *tell the full story*. The first automobile drivers were jeered. "Get a horse" was the cry, and it took a full explanation to convince the public that the car was really superior to the horse and buggy.

In the *competitive stage,* the product has been accepted as a good thing, and it now has many rivals. Here it is a question of *demonstrating the difference,* of showing why *our* brand is better than *their* brands.

In the *retentive stage,* there is no striking product differential. The market must be held, or extended, by *establishing a feeling* for the product. Ads for products in this stage frequently are short on copy, long on imagery. Retentive campaigns are designed to leave the consumer with a good, almost affectionate feeling about the product.

The stages are not always clear-cut; they may flow together, particularly the competitive and retentive stages. The campaign planners, however, must decide if they are after a new market, a share of competitors' market, or want to establish a firm hold on their present market, as it is unlikely that all three objectives could be reached in one campaign.

Deciding What to Say

The problem has been defined, the advertising objective formulated. The next step is to determine what to say. What you are looking for is a strong *concept.* The following ideas for copy approaches may be helpful in developing this aspect of the campaign.

Copy Approach: BRAND IMAGE related to consumer needs. What personality or brand image do you want to project for the product? What feeling do people now have about the product? What feeling do you want them to have about the product? In consumer product advertising, the brand image is always a part of your considerations. The brand image is not simply a picture. It is a picture in someone's mind. And this picture is usually created first of all with copy, a picture painted with words. The right words will elicit the right responses from the reader; the words aid recall and brand identification. Words contribute consciously or subconsciously to the feeling that the reader has about the brand, and that feeling is the *brand image.*

Pilot Life Insurance Company has a visual symbol of a sea captain behind the wheel of a ship. Relying on the symbol alone, one might logically conclude that the company insures sailors or that it writes marine insurance. But one does not rely on the symbol alone. The symbol is explained with words. It stands for steadfastness, it stands for experience, it stands for protection, it stands for safe guidance to the port of security. By associating the symbol with the appropriate copy, it becomes possible to show the symbol alone — and the viewer will respond with the proper feeling. His eyes see the picture; his mind supplies the words. The pilot behind the wheel stands for steadfastness, experience, protection, safe guidance. The brand image suggests the product, benefit, and name.

Other good and effective symbols which have contributed to a positive brand image are Lay Packing Company's *Three Little Pigs,* Green Giant Company's

Jolly Green Giant, Standard Oil Company's *Tiger,* and Cadillac's "extended V." Also, there are many excellent examples of pure design with interpretive values. In all cases, before the consumer makes a quick, correct response to the symbol, he will have been conditioned by the word pictures that have been painted in his mind.

This is only one way of creating a personality or brand image. There are other techniques. One is to exploit the personality of the maker. Early in the history of Eastern Airlines, its President, Eddie Rickenbacher, was featured in its ads. Because this great and famous aviator associated himself with the airline, it took on his image. A personal endorsement, in which the man stands behind his product, is especially good for a young company because it helps to gain consumer confidence.

If there is no paragon available to symbolize the product, consider inventing one, a person who will embody those qualities most likely to attract the prospects sought. The average homemaker, for instance, would be hard put to identify with a large company like General Mills, but she *can* identify with gracious, grey-haired Betty Crocker who, like the next-door neighbor, is always ready to share pet recipes and pass on household hints.

And what about the name of the product? Is it a strong name? Does it suggest the service of the product? The name should be suggestive of the benefit, but not descriptive, or it cannot be protected by a trademark registration. If the name lacks meaning, it might be well to pair it with a slogan that explains it. Names with no meaning take more time and money to establish than strong, suggestive names. What's in a name? Plenty, in advertising – the right name can tell a whole selling story.

There are many ways to build a personality for the product. The goal is to knowingly create a distinctive personality, one that will identify it and set it apart from its competitors. It must be a personality that fits the product and is readily understood by the prospect.

The expression of personality does not depend on style of writing alone. People's personalities are reflected by many things including dress, manners, and speech. So does the entire ad reflect the personality of the product. Concept, symbols, art work or photography, type, overall design – all help to create personality.

Once a pleasing product personality evolves, it is wise to stay with it, remaining consistent in looks, name, and style. When you change a product's personality, you are changing it from friend to stranger, and are asking your prospects to get reacquainted with it. (Would Schweppe's shave off the Commander's beard? Never!)

Copy Approach: PRODUCT BENEFIT related to consumer needs. What is the major benefit the product has to offer, and how may this benefit be interpreted in terms of the prospect's interest? Advertising for a New Car Savings Account at First Federal Savings and Loan Association gives the prospect a specific reason to buy. The ad points out that the account enables him to save enough money in interest alone to buy gas for a year – "Free gas for a year" is an example of interpreting the benefit in terms of the prospect's interest.

Frequently, the product can contribute to the solution of a special problem that the consumer has. If so, this must be proved and demonstrated. The important point is, it is self-interest, not philanthropy, that leads the consumer to buy. He wants to benefit from your product.

Be wary of undertaking to sell a concept that applies to *all* brands. Obviously, milk's major benefit is its health value, but if you settle on a Drink-Milk-For-Good-Health approach, you will be benefiting *all* brands of milk, not just your own brand, and this is a job for an association, not for you. What you will concentrate on is the major benefit of your own particular product.

Copy Approach: PRODUCT DIFFERENCE related to consumer needs. Is there a unique sales feature? What does your product have that your competition's doesn't have? Possibly the product has several singular features that might be combined into a single unique selling proposition. If there are several unusual sales features, which one is the most important? Which one is the strongest? Which one has not only immediate value, but also long range value? Which one can you build a campaign on?

Copy Approach: OVERCOMING OBJECTIONS related to consumer needs. Is there a major, or are there minor objections to the product? Can the objections be overcome? Find and present the positive side of an objection and convert it into a sales feature. Volkswagen has done an outstandingly successful job with this technique.

Copy Approach: FEATURE-FUNCTION-VALUE related to consumer needs. What feature-function-value does your product offer? This copy approach should be considered for industrial products or business goods. What is the main feature of the product or service? What other features are there? What is the function of each? What value do they have to the prospect? In industrial selling, the needs of the prospective manufacturer-customer are usually reasonably well defined. Therefore, if your product meets these needs and has features which make it stand out from others the manufacturer might consider, you will get your share of the business by building your sales talks around these points.

Relying on Marketing Research

Intuition and guesswork will not guide the planners through the conception of a campaign. There are many questions for which answers must be had. What *is* the product's major benefit? What *is* the prospect's problem? What *is* the strongest sales feature? Marketing research can be a reliable guide here. While it may not provide definite answers, it does reduce the possibility of error.

Marketing research refers us back to the Marketing Concept, the philosophy of business in which the product is seen through the eyes of the consumer. Marketing research will help to determine what customers want – and *don't* want. (You cannot be successful in trying to sell people what they do not want.) Ideas, appeals, and benefits should be tested on a cross-section of the market, either by mail or in person, before the ad campaign is approved and the money spent.

Testing done during a political campaign proves the value of marketing research, because the campaign is concentrated within a short, specified time period, and it is possible to measure end results against initial findings. A consumer campaign has no such short time limit and it is more difficult to judge exactly how well marketing research has done its job.

In a recent congressional election, we handled the campaign for one candidate. Several months before election day, an opinion poll was conducted on a systematic sampling basis. Our candidate won 32% of the popularity vote, while his major opponent won 40%. Voters were also questioned about the issues. The answers were compiled into 12 issues or "wants" and were made the basis of our candidate's campaign speeches.

Throughout the campaign, the issues were used in advertising and publicity, with emphasis on those that had received the most mention from the voters. As the campaign drew to a close, another opinion poll was conducted. This time, our candidate won 53% of the voters' favor and went on to win the election. The campaign had been seen through the eyes of the voters. By focusing on their "wants," the candidate was able to show his sincere concern and to pledge to do his best to fulfill those wants. Marketing research had shown the way. The same technique had been used in a preceding election to help elect a political newcomer a United States Senator.

After stating the problem, formulating the ad objective, and deciding *what* should be said, the copywriter's challenge becomes *how to say it* most effectively. Creativity is the process of finding the right answer.

Saying It: The Creative Presentation

Reduced to simple algebra, the equation for creative copywriting is $A + B = C$.

A is your knowledge of the product in relation to the problem and the objective.

B is the sum of all your other knowledge and experience, both contemporary and historical.

C is the creative concept – the "Big Idea," the answer. It is a unique but relevant way to tell the story.

The creative concept results from adding together in a new and meaningful relationship a known quantity, A, and a previously unrelated quantity drawn from other knowledge and experience, B. Scientists use the same equation, and they call their results inventions. Not all inventions are good. A good creative concept involves good judgment – the ability to select what is good and discard what is not.

Let's see how the equation $A + B = C$ worked out in the case of an ad campaign for one client, Pilot Life Insurance Company. The ad objective was to create greater *share of mind* for a multiple line of insurance coverages and, in so doing, to sell the total resourcefulness of the company for many different types of insurance needs – life insurance, group, hospitalization, major medical, business, retirement income, scholastic accident, and pension trusts. A complex and complicated product subject for an ad. Yet this was the known quantity, *A*. The unknown quantity, *B*, required a lot of digging. Since words and pictures are used in advertising, those involved in the creative process must be able to think verbally *and* visually. At least fifty ideas must have been considered before thinking up one that was fresh and meaningful. It had not been previously related to *A*, but could be, the only qualifying condition being to bring it off in good taste. Quantity *B* was an *egg*.

The egg idea came from a chance remark in a creative skull session that the insurance company's line of coverages was like a "Baker's Dozen." "Dozen" sparked "eggs." Eggs caricatured like people representing the prime markets for the various coverages became quantity *B*. A creative concept was born. The TV commercial that resulted won a national award. But, and this is even more important, it accomplished the ad objective with a high consumer recall rating.

Several years ago, our client, the Lay Packing Company, came out with a new sausage product which was named, forthrightly, Lay's All-Beef Franks. The problem was that there were a dozen brands of all-beef franks in the meat counter, and Lay's All-Beef Franks got lost in the crowd.

After a dismal sales period, the problem was thrown to the agency. We began with quantity *A*. What did we know about the product that related to the problem and the objective? We knew that it was an excellent, high-quality product that needed an appealing image. It needed a new name and a new package. We knew also that laboratory tests had shown that Lay's All-Beef Franks had a higher protein and a lower fat content than any sausage kitchen product in Lay's line. In fact, the franks had a higher protein and lower fat content than sirloin steak.

We read up on protein and found that it makes up 80% of the dry weight of muscle, 70% of the dry weight of skin, and 90% of the dry weight of blood. Protein is needed for growth, for strength, for health and, since it needs to be continually renewed, it is always essential in man's diet.

That brought us to quantity *B*, the previously unrelated quantity drawn from other knowledge. With what did we associate protein? Strong, healthy bodies. Physical health is associated with strenuous physical activity or sports. What rigorous sport would our market identify with best? Football. And there was a certain football term which, associated with our product, would not only suggest health and strength but also give it the connotation of being a winner. The term was *touchdown.* And the marriage of the two (A + B) was *C*, the creative concept.

Lay's All-Beef Franks were re-christened Lay's Touchdown Franks. The new package design had a football look to coordinate with the new name and was in football colors (orange and white) that need no

explanation in this marketing area. We also went from
ten franks in the package to eight, which made for a
bigger, beefier wiener, and put a premium price on the
product.

Touchdown Franks really scored for Lay's. The
response to the product's new personality was
immediate and favorable. Sales went up and have
continued to go up each year. Touchdown Franks are
one of Lay's best sellers. Where once the product was
"a bench warmer" in their lineup, it is now a star.

Saying It: The Creative Product

In the creative ad, the product is seen in a new
light, in a new relationship that is relative to the
product and the prospect.

There is a distinction that should be made. Not
all advertising has to be creative in the above sense to
be effective. In fact, there are times when it is better
for the ad not to be so. This is true when the product
itself is highly creative – that is, when the product is a
new idea (a blending of *A* and *B*), or when the
product has a new and beneficial feature. This is when
"news" of the *creative product* presented in an
interesting manner will communicate more directly
and meaningfully. To add a highly creative ad
presentation to the creative idea of the product may
compound the communications problem. When there
is a question here, it is wiser to select the simpler,
more direct approach.

The effective ad, no matter whether it is the
product or the presentation that is creative, is the one

that reveals a truth about the product that the prospect can instantly understand and believe because it is presented in terms of real life experience. The prospect loses patience with advertising that strikes him as unreal, that is not tied to his own situation and to his own knowledge of the product. The effective ad gives the prospect what he is looking for – honest information.

Creativity is not what you *do* on Thursday after defining the problem on Monday, formulating the ad objective on Tuesday, and deciding on the copy approach on Wednesday. "The creative artist," John Dewey said, "unites the old and the new in a 'quick and unexpected harmony.' But it is not a spontaneous process. Neither is it random."[1] In other words, there is much to be done before the "quick and unexpected harmony" can be achieved.

Knowing the Product and the Prospects

The most important element in the ad is the product itself, so you must know all there is to know about it. Your research will include your competitors' products, for you are not only selling your product, you are also selling against competing products.

You know the product. But you must also know the people to whom you are selling it and why they would be interested in it. Here you need facts, experience, and exposure to life because when you sit down to write the ad, you must have a picture of the

[1] John Dewey, "Surge in Creativity: Is Intuition the Key," *Printer's Ink Basic Checklist and Idea Book* (1962), p. 171.

prospect in your mind. You must understand and take his point of view. If you are writing to an engineer, talk to engineers. Read some books on engineering. Learn how an engineer thinks and reacts. If you are writing to a housewife, spend some time in the kitchen, mind the kids, learn the housewives' problems, watch the TV shows they watch, read the magazines they read. You have to be curious about life. Be as thorough in your analysis of the market as you are in your analysis of the product.

Before you can decide what you want to say, you must be thoroughly familiar with product and prospect. In the last analysis, it is the content of the ad, not the form, that will cause the prospect to buy or not to buy. What you say comes first; how you say it comes second. And content, to a large degree, depends on knowledge of product and prospect.

Let's say that you've settled on your approach; you have decided what is worth saying and how to say it. Now the time has come to write the ad. It's up to you at this point. Committees may suggest, recommend, and criticize, but they don't (or shouldn't) write ads. A communal effort is likely to lack style, coherence, and harmony. Copywriting at its best is an individual effort.

Your product may have a large market, but you never try to communicate with a mass audience. Your ad isn't an oration, it is immediate and intimate person-to-person selling. Although you want to reach many persons, you write to only one, a typical prospect.

So consider the lady under the hair dryer. There she sits, your Mrs. Consumer. She has a glossy women's magazine on her lap and she is blissfully anticipating thirty minutes of solitude and the chance to catch up on her reading. She's looking forward to the current feature story on some personality in the news; there's an article on cruelty in the maternity wards that has caught her eye; she has high hopes for a series of recipes grouped under the heading "Glamorize the Humble Squash" (maybe the kids will eat it if she prepares it a new way). Notice that she isn't *planning* to read any ads. But she will. A few will stop her because they have something to do with her and with her life, because they provoke her curiosity and arouse her interest to such an extent that she pauses, involuntarily, to read them. Will your ad be one of them?

Your first job is to call to her, to flag her down as she passes by your ad to get to her feature story. Before you can speak to her directly in the headline, you must halt her. This is where the total look of the ad is important.

Total Look of the Ad

You decide on your format after you have decided on your ad concept, your "Big Idea." There are two presentation techniques which have proved to be above average attention-getters. These you will need to discuss with your Art Director. One is to be "with the book." Readership studies show that editorial content enjoys a higher readership, on the average, than advertising. Being "with the book" means using a distinctive editorial that has the appearance of an authoritative article. An ad that doesn't look like an ad can have attention value akin to that which a news story receives.

The second technique for attracting attention (and the one most frequently used) is to be "against the book." If the format of the ad is markedly different from the editorial format and from the format of other advertisers, you have built-in extra attention value. Almost every year we see a few totally new formats or a new art technique, photographic technique, or a new type face associated with a product that is enjoying outstanding marketing success. But successful innovation leads to imitation. Soon other advertisers are copying these styles. Then the attention value is diluted, and the challenge is to come up with something new.

Your format, the total look of your ad, stops your prospect, the lady under the hair dryer. The next two or three seconds are crucial. Will she stay with you and read the ad, or will she turn the page?

How do people read ads, anyway? How do *you* read an ad? Research indicates pretty clearly that most people will scan an ad before reading it. In scanning an ad, they notice the most visual elements: the *illustration,* the *headline,* and the *logotype* if it is prominent. On the average, only one in five who scans the ad and reads the headline will be interested enough in the proposition to read the body copy.

Common sense indicates that the product, the brand name, and the benefit should be memorably presented in the three most visual elements.

If the product is prominent in the illustration, the name need not be in the headline, but may be.

If the product is not prominent in the illustration, the name should either be in the headline or in a logo.

If the product name is neither in the headline nor the illustration, a product logo is required.

If product identification is strong in either the headline or the illustration, a small logo, or even no logo, is permissible.

Many young writers and designers fail to reason this out. They frequently over-commercialize (too much product identification) and their ads lack good taste, or they under-commercialize (no product picture, no product name in the headline, no product logo) and waste 80% of the advertiser's money.

Guidelines for Writing the Ad

Now, about actually writing the ad. Guidelines based on experience and study may be established, but firm rules for ad writing are limiting because methods of presentation change with the times. There are fashions in advertising as there are in anything else, and today's "with it" ad will, with the passage of time, look as dated as the bustle and the Model T. In 1926, "literary" copy was considered creative advertising. The author of a book called *The Language of Advertising* held the following copy up as a model for aspiring copywriters:

> "Now, over the way at your grocer's, these Three Good Spirits dwell today – in a fairy box of a new kind of corn flakes named *Quaker Quakies.*
>
> "And, Oh, what different corn flakes are these *Quaker Quakies.* So full of strength for little bodies! So full of brave color for little cheeks! So full of true thoughts for little hearts and minds!"[1]

This Granny Sweetpants style of writing, so admirable then, wouldn't sell a six-year old today.

Today's market is better educated, less credulous, and more critical than ever before, and it is probably easier to write a news story than it is to write an ad. An account of a movie star's sixth divorce will be of innate interest to the lady under the hair dryer. It requires no ingenuity on the writer's part to make the story interesting to her; all that is necessary is to report the facts. On the other hand, writing an ad requires a great deal of ingenuity. You must tell the story of your product in only one or two hundred words and, at the same time, tell it in such a way that you will arouse and hold the reader's interest – and also make it stand out from competing ads.

Hard sell won't reach the lady under the hair dryer because she's heard all that before. She's tired of drum rolls and trumpet flourishes; she doesn't believe

---

[1] John B. Opdycke, *The Language of Advertising* (New York: Pitman and Sons, 1926), p. 253.

all that fanfare (here comes THE PRODUCT, it was perfect before, but now it is NEW, IMPROVED, BETTER THAN EVER, DON'T DELAY, BUY NOW!). Loud, insistent ads will repel the reader. Soft sell won't reach her, either. She's being assailed on all sides by advertisements, and she's developed a protective armor which soft sell won't penetrate.

What you are after is "deep sell" that goes in and stays. How do you create deep sell? To begin with, your *ad theme should be different.* Check to see what the competition has done and is doing. If there is similarity, effectiveness will be diminished. If your theme is original, effectiveness will be enhanced.

Your ad should be *contemporary.* A contemporary ad has a voice. It isn't *written.* It *speaks.* It has the candor, the immediacy, and the informality of person-to-person communication. As you write, imagine how you would explain, verbally, the benefits of the product to a friend. Use the everyday words and the unstudied phrases that make up ordinary conversation. But mind you, what seems as effortless and spontaneous as speech is actually the result of a planned informality. An informality that moves naturally and inevitably from beginning to middle to end because it has been carefully plotted and concentrated to make every word count. This is a technique which produces an ad that is personal, direct, real — easy to read, easy to understand, and easy to believe.

Television has had a great deal to do with the evolution of the print-ad-with-a-voice. Because of the prospect's exposure to television, she has been conditioned to *hearing* advertising. If, as she reads your ad, she *hears* as well as *sees* the words, you have succeeded in transferring the sound of television to print, and your ad is contemporary.

And then there are certain appeals which will strike a responsive chord in the reader because they are *compatible with basic human psychology.* Styles may change, but certain characteristics of people do not change. The appeal to the reader's self-interest will always appear in any effective ad. Do not ask the lady under the hair dryer to buy; ask her to benefit herself.

Another appeal that works is to *invite comparison.* Ask your prospect to judge for herself (with samples, free demonstrations, trial offers, guarantees). This shows that you respect her desire for high quality and performance and that you have enough confidence in your product to let it be tested.

If you must make *claims, back them up.* Do not say, "The Chocomarsh-Nuttycrunch Bar contains more nuts than any candy bar on the market." Say, "Laboratory tests prove that the (Maker's Name) Chocomarsh-Nuttycrunch Bar contains 7% more almonds and 11% more peanuts than any candy bar on the market." Use tests and research to document your claims. Proven facts and figures are convincing.

Surprise-Appropriateness-Memorability

Strive to be contemporary and to appeal to what is basic in human nature. And, if your ad concept is to be presented effectively, your ad will contain a high degree of these three factors: Surprise, Appropriateness, Memorability.

What is surprise? Well, obviously, it is the unexpected. Something out of the ordinary. It might be understatement, as in the case of the Volkswagen ad that told the reader to "THINK SMALL." Surprising – we're used to being told to "think big." But add the words to the picture of the little bug and they make sense. Think *small*; consider the advantages of owning this car. Surprise might be reverse psychology, as in the Avis car rental ad, "WE ARE ONLY NUMBER 2." Why so modest? Why call attention to the fact that you're only second best? Because "WE TRY HARDER"; the underdog, naturally, wants to be top-dog.

Surprise might be incongruity – a fat woman in a girdle ad instead of the fashion model you would expect to see. Surprise could be achieved through the use of such rhetorical devices as the metaphor or simile in which a likeness is noted between two seemingly unrelated and unlike objects. In the case of a food product, surprise could mean making the product look more appetizing than would normally be expected.

Surprise is being different. It should jar the reader out of her indifference and involve her in the ad. But what adds to the impact and strengthens the interest and appeal of the ad is the reader's immediate realization that the surprise is also *appropriate.* It must relate to the product, to the user of the product, and to the benefit the product offers. It must fit the selling idea.

Suppose your mother-in-law biked across the country on a Honda and turned up on your doorstep wearing a crash helmet, a Batman T-shirt, jeans, and knee-high white boots. That would be surprising. In fact, the kids would be much more interested in the Honda and the crazy clothes than in Grandma herself. In the same way, many ad makers (unsuccessfully imitating successful ads) hide their product's good qualities under an eccentric presentation in which surprise is used for its own sake, thereby sacrificing effectiveness.

Which brings us to the third factor, *memorability*. You are competing for a *share of mind*. In addition to being noted, the ad must be remembered. Bill Bernbach of Doyle Dane Bernbach, a highly creative advertising man, emphasizes that what should be memorable in the ad is "the advantage of our product."[1] This goes back to the first law of advertising, *advertising is selling*. What you are after in an ad is not to make the prospect remember that beautiful photograph or that witty headline, but to make him remember the specific advantage that your product offers him. A memorable ad, Bill Bernbach says, must be "fresh and original." If you have surprise, justified by appropriateness, it is likely that your ad *will* be fresh, original, and memorable.

The Headline

Back to that typical prospect, the lady under the hair dryer. After she scans the ad, glancing at its major elements, she focuses on the headline and illustration.

[1] William Bernbach, "Research, Marketing Alone Can't Make Good Advertising," *Advertising Age* (February 1, 1960), p. 77.

They are the *most important elements* in the ad; 80% of the client's money goes into the headline and the illustration. When you have written your headline and composed your illustration, you have spent 80 cents of your dollar.

Not everyone will be interested in reading your ad. People are selective in their reading; they do not have the time to be otherwise. Your headline *should select your chosen audience* by featuring the benefit which will have the strongest appeal to that audience.

In the case of a specialized product, your readership will be limited to a specialized market. For example, a headline for a food supplement intended to put weight on thin people will naturally select skinny readers.

But what if your product has a tremendous market? A drug product, for example. The product has both a health and a beauty benefit. Suppose that research has shown that 60% of users look for a health benefit in this type of product, while 40% look for a beauty benefit. Suppose there are 10 brands on the market. Seven appeal to the health benefit in their advertising. Two appeal to beauty benefit. How should you go? If you go the "health benefit" route, you have a theoretical potential of 1/8 of 60%, or 7½% share of market, if all brands are equal. If you go the "beauty benefit" route, your "fair share" potential is 1/3 of 40% or 13-1/3% share of market. Would it be better strategy, then, to aim at the minority, the beauty seekers? A smaller market with less competition gives you a chance at better response. In other words, from a vast audience, you must decide which group you want to appeal to, and then write your headline to select that particular group. A headline that tries to appeal to everyone is doomed to appeal to no one; you cannot be all things to all people. Your headline must telegraph what you want to say, and telegraph it in plain language. The lady under the hair dryer will listen politely when she is button-holed by a bore at a party, but good manners and etiquette do not apply to ad reading, and she can go off and leave you whenever she wants to leave you. If the headline bores her or confuses her, if it does not make sense at once, if it is in poor taste, if it is irrelevant, if it doesn't offer her anything, she *will* leave you.

What makes a good headline? A headline that contains *an appeal to the reader's self-interest.* She is interested in the product only as it relates to her. The *promise of a benefit* will draw her into the ad. A headline that contains *news* makes a good headline. The consumer is always on the lookout for new products, new ways to use old products, or improvements in products. A headline that *arouses curiosity* also makes a good headline; it will lure your prospect into reading on.

There are two obvious "don'ts" in headline writing.

First, don't write a headline that says something different from what the illustration shows. It will cause confusion and a breakdown in communication with the reader. Your ability to visualize should prevent your making this error. A copywriter must see the ad as an entity, not just as words (*his* creation) which must be combined with several other elements (someone else's creation) that, because they are not his primary responsibility, are shadowy in his mind. From the ad's inception, you should see it as a whole so that all elements are compatible and are coordinated to complement each other to give full force to the sales message. (In some instances, when the picture can tell the story better than words can, the wise copywriter uses the picture and eliminates the words.)

Second, don't write an irrelevant headline. As we have pointed out already, only one out of five who read the headline will go on to read the body copy. A headline that can't stand alone, that means nothing by itself, accomplishes nothing with those four out of five who don't read the whole ad. An irrelevant headline wastes your opportunity to reach them.

Body Copy

We will assume that so far your ad is irresistible and that your headline acts like a magnet on the prospect, drawing her into the body copy. She will read it because the headline and illustration have, most persuasively, held out a promise to her; now she wants to find out how the product can fulfill its promise. She wants information and ideas, presented in a clear and lively fashion.

The story that you tell in your ad should be structured to win these five responses from your reader: *attention, interest, desire, conviction, action.*

The headline, of course, is where you attract attention by featuring your most important benefit positively – or negatively, if you are using the problem-solution format.

Your first paragraph should *build interest by relating the appeal of the benefit to the reader* and by beginning to enlarge on the benefit. The opening paragraph should be short and direct, with a minimum of words. The reader will find a long first paragraph tedious; she may wonder when, if ever, you are going to get to the point; she may lose interest altogether and read no further.

Next, you will *build desire by being specific.* Tell the reader exactly what she will get. Infinite detail is not necessary. Be concise, be truthful, be interesting. Stay away from superlatives and generalizations. If you have a lot of unrelated facts that you believe are indispensable, don't try to tie them together in an awkward paragraph. Simply number and list them.

When you have built desire, you must *reinforce it with conviction.* The reader must believe you. Offer proof in some form that the product really does perform as you have promised it will – endorsements, testimonials from satisfied users, "third party statements," laboratory tests, and "happy endings." You may even mention possible loss of something the prospect values, like lustrous hair, without use of your product.

Finally, you reach the point of *inducing action.* Rephrase the prominent benefit that you offered at the beginning of the ad, and tell the reader how to act (unless it is obvious). Give the reader an incentive to act, a "reason to buy."

Visually Punctuate Your Ad

Throughout the ad, use short paragraphs, short sentences, short words. Punctuate it visually so it is easy to read. This doesn't mean, of course, that the ad you produce should read like a first grade primer. Yes, your words should be easy to understand. Yes, your words should convey the message as simply and as directly as possible. But a short word is not necessarily a dull word. The English language contains a rich and complete assortment of short words that have clarity, color, and connotation. It is your business to use them.

We'll say that your ad has every creative advertising virtue in the book. It is fresh, original, memorable, and believable. It has surprise. It has a message and a promise. The headline is provocative. The body copy is clear, factual, and fun. The ad puts a favorable idea about the product into your prospect's head. A sale may result.

The Case for Consistency and Repetition

But how long will the reader remember your ad? Isn't there a possibility that before she acts on it, another advertising story may crowd it out of her mind? (We're not speaking here of *share of market* advertising, which hits hard for an immediate sale with promotional offers, but of *share of mind* advertising which aims at securing brand loyalty in order to achieve a consistently high sales record.)

Several years ago, the Ted Bates Agency conducted a study to determine the life expectancy of what it termed *penetration* — the number of people who do (or do not) remember a campaign, once they have it in their heads.

The agency found out the exact number of people who remembered its advertising of a big brand. Fifty per cent remembered it; fifty per cent did not. The names and addresses of these people were recorded, and six months later the agency went back to them. The same campaign was still running. Half of the people who *had* known the ad story had forgotten it. Half of those who *had not* known it six months before could now describe it.[1]

The study makes a strong case for *consistency of copy story in a long-range ad campaign program.* The prolonged use of a good selling story increases its effectiveness; six months after it appears, it is still reaching prospects.

Suppose that your reader is only going to remember your ad for six months. During that time, she may or may not buy the product. If she does buy it, your ad will be of no further interest to her because her desire for the product has been satisfied. During the same period, however, another consumer will enter the picture. The circumstances of her life have put her in the market for the product.

David Ogilvy expresses it this way:

You aren't advertising to a standing

[1] Rosser Reeves, *Reality in Advertising* (New York: Alfred A. Knopf, 1961), p. 25.

> army; you are advertising to a moving
> parade. Three million consumers get
> married every year...one million, seven
> hundred consumers die every year, and
> four million new ones are born. They
> enter the market and they depart from
> it. An advertisement is like a radar
> sweep, constantly hunting new
> prospects as they come into the
> market.[1]

An unpublished study made by McGraw-Hill
Publishing Company shows that the same holds true in
the industrial market; it, too, is a "moving parade."
Each year, the study revealed, out of every 1,000
industrial personnel, only 504 stay in the same job,
the same company, the same location; 54 change
titles, 140 are transferred, 302 are replaced. The ad
campaign for the industrial product, like the campaign
for the consumer product, is continually reaching new
prospects.

Your ad theme should be worthy of repetition.
A good ad, a creative ad, is one that is good now and
six months from now. It reaches the moving parade of
consumers, and it builds a definite personality for the
product. A friend is someone whose personality
pleases us; so must a product's personality please the
consumer. A pleasing personality will bring the
product into the consumer's life – and keep it there.

---

[1] David Ogilvy, *Confessions of an Advertising Man* (New York: Atheneum, 1963), p. 99.

CHAPTER SUMMARY

The Ad Man as a Copywriter

Before he writes the ad —

He knows the problem.

He knows the objective.

He is familiar with market and product research that will help him decide what should be said.

He knows the formula for creativity — how to say it.

When he writes the ad —

He knows the product, the prospect, the objective, and the creative concept.

He writes to one person.

He appeals to basic human psychology, giving the prospect a "reason to buy."

He documents claims with facts.

He strives to be contemporary and different.

He makes the advantage of the product memorable.

He telegraphs the sales message to a selected audience with his headline.

He builds interest and desire and induces action with his body copy.

He is satisfied that the theme is worthy of repetition in order to reach the "moving" parade" of potential buyers.

6
The
ad man
as an
art director

The Ad Man as an Art Director

Men have used pictures to express ideas and emotions since the Stone Age. Much has changed in art style, technique, and form since the time when men drew crude but graphic pictures on the walls of caves, but the primary goal remains the same – to communicate with visual symbols.

All art may be said to be concerned with the arrangement of forms into a composition, but from there on fine art and commercial art take divergent paths. The painter works alone; his paintings are personal and subjective. He paints to fulfill his need to make his ideas visual, and he hopes that his view of life and the world will have meaning to others. The commercial artist works with others to communicate not a personal idea, but an idea about a product. He must present in pictures the same concept that the copywriter has presented in words. Words and illustrations complement each other; together they form a pleasing picture of the product in the consumer's mind.

The art director is concerned with the visual illustration of the advertising message and with the layout which is the arrangement of the elements.

Lead Considerations

As background to preparing the visual illustration and the layout, you must understand the *objectives of the ad* — what it is the ad is to accomplish. You must learn about the *product,* how it is sold, and for how much it is sold. If it is a package goods item sold in self-service stores, the package takes on increased importance. How much attention should be given to the package or to the logotype in the ad?

You will add knowledge of the *prospect* to your knowledge of the product. You will want to know what type of people the ad is to reach and what *media* will be used to reach them. The media will influence the layout or design. Newspapers, printed on porous, inexpensive paper, are generally characterized by busy pages and hurried readership. For these reasons, it is usually preferable to design the ad within a white margin or frame on all four sides, so that it will separate and stand out from competing items on the page. Oversize type, white space, dominant illustrations, or other devices aid in achieving strong contrast.

Magazine readership is more leisurely, and reproduction is on high grade paper. Quality and appearance are lead considerations. There will be few, if any, other ads on the average page, so you can be "quieter" and more effective. Taste, in relation to the publication, is an important factor.

How People Read Ads

In designing advertising it is important to know something of how people read ads. Many qualified studies of ad readership have been made over the years. While results will vary with media and the size of the ads, the preponderance of evidence indicates the following characteristics:

For every 120 people "reading" the illustration, 100 people will read the headline, 108 the signature, 30 the picture caption, and 10 the body copy.

In many good ads, elements are combined. Where the product signature is featured in the illustration, this results in the two "most read" units being one element. Also, the headline may serve as the picture caption, further reducing the number of elements and clutter.

If outdoor is to be the medium, the problem requires a different approach. The short reading time of an outdoor poster calls for brevity and maximum simplicity. The fewer words of copy the better, if they tell the story (five to ten words). Ideally, the layout should be reduced to one element plus the logo for best comprehension. Two elements, however, are more common, and three are permissible if handled properly. Never more. The picture usually does the major selling job. Type is kept simple and easy to read at a distance. Color is important. It may be used to attract attention, create emotional response, beautify the product image, and to accomplish almost every other desirable objective.

Other Considerations

The art director and the copy director (copywriter) usually work together in conceiving the

ad. After the concept has been determined and the
first draft of the copy has been written, he begins his
layout. Final form of the copy may be different,
because the picture may eliminate the need for some
of the words or may require a change in arrangement.
The art director and the copywriter will work closely
together to achieve the union of words and illustration
which will best express the ad concept. Frequently,
the copywriter will have some ideas for visual
expression which he will pass on to the art director.

The art director must also know what method of
reproduction is to be used (letterpress, offset
lithography, gravure, silk screen), for this will have a
bearing on the many choices he must make as he plans
the illustration and layout.

It is up to the art director to decide whether to
use photography or art work. The photograph can do
it faster, make the subject more timely, and save
money. The photograph is reality; it is believable; it is
immediate. It may be used in an infinite variety of
ways. For example, a photograph of a seemingly
impossible situation creates a kind of magic realism
that is an attention-getter. And there are many
photomechanical techniques with which an art director
should be familiar so that he will know when and how
to use the appropriate one to achieve a special effect
for the ad.

The many modern art forms, however, are able
to communicate in new and effective ways so that art
work can, in many instances, meet the challenge of
photography. There are many mediums – pen and ink,

wash drawings, crayon, drybrush — each with its own special quality. Again, it is a matter of selecting the right one to achieve desired effects in the ad.

In making the choice between art work and photography, the art director will consider time, cost, competition for attention, believability, and image. The method of reproduction will influence his choice. But, above all, he must consider the communication value of his selection. Is it the one that will tell the story most effectively?

The Concept Sketch

The art director approaches the ad as a designer with the prime purpose of communicating an idea. The end result of the ad — art and copy — will be the painting of a picture in somebody's mind.

First sketches will be concerned with *concept,* making the headline idea visual. Aside from color and size, the most important characteristic of the ad layout in stopping readers is a *dominant focal center.* In picture, type, or both, the focal center is the equivalent of the illustration. The purpose of the illustration is to portray consumer needs and product benefits in the sales message. The sales message is what you want the prospect to notice and remember. Headline and copy contain a sales message; so should the illustration — the *same* sales message.

The illustration should normally show one or more of the following:

    1. The product in use, or perhaps in a setting to enhance its image.

2. The symbol of the product.

3. The benefit of the product.

4. The problem that the product can help solve.

5. The market that the product serves.

The Rough Layout

The visualization or *concept* sketch is next incorporated in a rough layout with all of the elements that go into the ad — headline, subheads, body copy, supplementary illustrations, logo, etc.

The rough layout is then ready to be evaluated from the following standpoints:

1. **Is the emphasis right?** Does the layout "fit" the product and the market? Is the appeal to the reader's self-interest, his "reason to buy," immediately apparent?

2. **Is the image right?** Does it express the product's personality? The layout should suggest the quality or qualities that characterize the product, such as economy, high style, cleanliness, appetite appeal, speed, comfort, safety, etc.

3. **Does the ad hold together as a unit?** The art director must have an aptitude for simplification, for the audience will not notice, let alone remember, all of the advertising to which it is exposed. He should give special attention to the possibility of combining or eliminating elements in order to reduce clutter and improve readability and impact. The ad should read easily and logically, the graphic balance should be

pleasing, and the type face should be simple and appropriate. Each element of the ad plays a part in building personality and in delivering the sales message. For example, the right type face (the *look* of a word) can actually convey sense and sound.

4. **Does the ad have sufficient attention value?** Is it visually unique; is it different? Will it catch, hold, and please the eye of the beholder? This is vital to the success of the ad, for if it lacks distinction, it will be lost in the crowd. The need to be different, however, does not give license to be "way out." The visual presentation must relate directly to the ad concept, to the product, and to the prospect's experience of life; and it must be in good taste. The ad should be different *and* appropriate.

The Finished Layout

After the rough layout is edited, the finished layout is done. It is usually prepared to actual size. The layout is valuable for several reasons. It shows the agency and the client how the completed ad will look. It is used to estimate cost. And it serves as a blueprint for all those who will contribute to the mechanical work involved in the production of the ad. The more comprehensive the layout, the better it will fulfill its functions. A comprehensive layout saves time and money at the printer's and is insurance against costly changes during production.

It is plainly evident that the task of art director will involve endless decisions and choices made for both esthetic and technical reasons. A thorough knowledge of production methods and costs will serve you well.

Package Design

Approach package design in much the same way that you approach the ad layout. Points of emphasis must be clearly outlined. Besides being a protective device, the package is an advertising medium, one of the best at point of sale. *Design of the package and, if possible, the selection of the brand name and trademark should be handled under the supervision of (or in concert with) the advertising agency.* The package and the advertising should work together, reinforcing each other. The advertising that reaches the consumer plays back to her when she sees the package in the store.

The brand name should be dominant. Colors should complement and heighten appeal of the product. The brand name should be easily recognized and readable at "display" distance. It should be simple, uncluttered, and in good taste.

The package should give information about contents, weight, and size and should give instructions on proper use. Space for pricing must be prominent. Federal and state regulations specify where many of these elements should be placed, and sometimes the regulations even specify the type size that must be used. Check all these details carefully before proceeding.

Corporate Design

The art director may have a responsibility in another area, that of corporate design in which graphics are used to build the *company image.* Large corporations, once faceless giants to the public, have established personalities for themselves through the use of graphics. Dr. Frank Stanton, president of CBS, has said, "I think there are few needs greater for the modern, large-scale corporation than the need for a broad public awareness of its personality — its sense of values. Increasingly, I think modern corporations are recognizing the high cost of impersonality...we believe that we should not only be progressive but *look* progressive."[1]

Almost every company, no matter what its size, is giving (or should give) increased attention to the face that it presents to the public. The way people feel about a company is often influenced by an image retained from past experience or exposure. It is not easy to replace this retained image with a new and broader vision; it means altering established patterns of thinking and feeling.

The design that symbolizes the company's personality will be carried through on packaging, advertising, letterheads, brochures, labels, and annual reports. What makes good corporate design?

1. It should express the personality of the company as it is now and

---

[1] Frank Stanton, "The Graphic Art of Corporate Image," Fortune (July, 1967), p. 127.

as it will be in the years
immediately ahead.

2. It should be esthetically and
   emotionally pleasing.
3. It should say exactly and concisely
   what you want said, so that it will
   communicate effectively.
4. It should have integrity.
5. It should be in good taste.
6. It should be contemporary. This
   does not mean modern. It means
   real, believable, in tune with what
   is happening today.
7. It should be as simple as possible
   but not lacking in any of the
   above qualities.
8. It should be distinctive.

Art for Advertising's Sake

In summary, the art director is not creating art
for art's sake, but art for advertising's sake. In the
world of advertising and business, the art director's
work is interrelated with the work of others – the
copywriter, the artists who work with him, and people
who attend to the technical end of producing an ad.
The art director must understand copy and concept so
that he is able to collaborate with the copywriter, for
words are very much a part of the picture in
advertising art. He must be able to interpret ideas to

those who work with him. And he must have a sound knowledge of printing and production.

Last, but by no means least, he will champion the cause of the high quality ad. He knows that a well-done ad in a half or three-quarter page size can out-produce a full page ad of less accomplished execution.

There are some advertisers who would sacrifice quality for quantity. They want the maximum amount of space or time and fail to allocate sufficient funds for art, production, or film. No matter how creative and ingenious the art director is, no matter how skilled he is at making good use of the most economical production methods, it is impossible to overcome the obstacles set up by a budget that is inadequate. In truth, the creative content and production quality of the ad represent 95% of its effectiveness. The only thing that makes space or time a good buy is a good idea well executed to go in it.

So the art director does his best to sell the idea of budgeting first what it will take to produce the best ads and then buying exposures in time and space with what is left over. A cheap job can end by being expensive if it does not produce the desired result. It is more desirable to make a first-rate impression on a few than a second-rate impression (or none at all) on many.

CHAPTER SUMMARY

The Ad Man as an Art Director

He communicates an idea about the product through a visual illustration of the advertising message.

He understands the objective, product, prospect, and creative concept.

He understands the different approaches required by the different media.

He works with the copywriter to express the ad concept.

He decides whether to use art work or photography.

He makes a *concept* sketch.

He does the layout and helps to evaluate it.

He has a working knowledge of production methods and techniques so he can assist in the mechanical end of the job.

He champions the cause of the high quality ad.

7
The
ad man as a
production
manager

The Ad Man as a Production Manager

The production manager's job is a vital one in the ad agency. He is, in a manner of speaking, the third member of a trio. The copywriter and the art director create print media; the production manager sees to its completion. After the artwork has been completed, it is the production manager who directs the work of engravers, printers, and other suppliers. The job calls for thoroughness, careful attention to detail, efficiency, and a tremendous reservoir of specialized knowledge.

In association with the art director, the production manager has the responsibility for manufacturing decisions. He serves as purchasing agent, and in most instances as traffic manager. At the start of each job, he will need to know the ad objective, the budget, and the deadline. The cost of work to be done may vary widely; obviously, a Cadillac cannot be produced at Chevy prices. Materials and suppliers are selected on the basis of objective, budget, and deadline.

The production manager needs to have a sound, practical knowledge of the components of a "print" ad — type, printing, engraving, paper, etc. — and how they work together. The following basic information can only begin to suggest the extent and complexity of the knowledge required to get the job done effectively.

TYPE CONSIDERATIONS

Let's begin by considering type. Type is what makes the impression on paper, and the various faces are classified according to class, style, size, width, and heaviness of tone. There are three commonly used methods of setting type: metal, photo composition, and pasteup type.

Metal

Metal type may be set in four ways. *Hand-set* is the most expensive, and it is usually limited to headlines and subheads. There is a large variety of faces and sizes available. *Monotype* is machine set with each letter cast individually and arranged in words or lines on a galley (or type tray). It is most commonly used for headlines or technical texts. *Ludlow* is a method in which hand-set matrices are assembled in a type stick and then cast as a unit. It is not as expensive as monotype to set, but it is less flexible for spacing or corrections. *Linotype,* or *Intertype,* is machine-set on a keyboard (like a typewriter) which activates matrices of each letter. They are then arranged in a "line of type" and cast. This is the cheapest method and is preferred for body copy and many subheads.

Photo Composition

Photo composition is the newest method of typesetting and has grown rapidly in acceptance. It offers the typesetter a lower equipment cost for a wide variety of contemporary typefaces. Special lenses can distort film type so that it can be made wider, narrower, or even curved. For special headings and trade names, it has, for all practical purposes, replaced hand lettering and metal type.

Photo composition may be used for headings, subheads, and body copy at prices comparable to metal type. In book composition, computer type (a form of photo composition) is today more efficient and less costly. The advantages of this method lie in the greater variety of faces and special sizes. The main disadvantage, especially in text or body copy, is in making corrections. Photo composition on tabular matter should be avoided.

Pasteup

Pasteup type is a handy aid for quick, low-budget jobs. Fonts of individual letters on transparent sheeting are available for very little cost. The letters can be assembled rapidly to set headlines or display features. The earlier pasteup type fonts were produced on individual cardboard strips and were set in much the same way as hand-set metal type. Later advances brought adhesive-backed cutout lettering into widespread use. Today, the most popular pasteup type is the "pressure-transfer" variety, where a burnishing tool is used to transfer an extremely thin Mylar letter from its backing sheet to the repro copy.

Selection of Typeface

Selection of typeface is important. Some type-faces are neutral, but many have certain personality characteristics. A typeface may be bold, dignified, modern, old-fashioned, rugged, delicate, stately, fast-moving ... There are three general categories of basic letter forms: serif (or Roman), sans-serif (or block), script and ornamental. Within these groups there are literally thousands of typefaces.

In making the layout, the art director has already indicated a style of typeface and arrangement that is an integral part of the overall design. As production manager, you will want to consult with him in selecting the exact typeface and size to complement the layout, keeping in mind these criteria:

1. Be sure the type is easy to read.
2. Select type that is appropriate to the message. If one is not available, use a neutral face.
3. Your ad will look better and be easier to read if you use a minimum of typefaces (perhaps one for the heading and one for the body copy).
4. Type arrangement should be orderly. It aids reading and also suggests a better quality product.

Typesetting Terms

Typesetting has its own language. The size of type is measured in *points* from the height of ascenders to descenders. There are 72 points to an inch. This book is set in 11 point type. The length of the type line is measured in *picas.* There are 6 picas to an inch. Spacing between lines of type is called *leading* and is measured in points.

After the type has been ordered, received, and proofread, it will be assembled along with the art and photographs into a *pasteup.* This mechanical assembly and positioning is critical, for it will influence the ultimate appearance of the ad or printed piece. Because halftones (photos or artwork with varying intensities of gray or black) and line art (such as type) are copied differently at the engravers or printers, the pasteup will have windows and overlays for positioning the various elements. How the "ad" is to be reproduced can influence details of how mechanicals are assembled.

PRINTING

After the ad is made up, it will be published by one of four methods of reproduction: letterpress, offset lithography, intaglio (or gravure), or silkscreen.

Letterpress

Letterpress printing is from a raised surface on which ink has been applied by a roller. The raised type and plate surfaces come in contact with the paper and make the impression. Letterpress traditionally has been most commonly used in magazine and newspaper reproduction; however, many have turned to offset printing as a less expensive method with greater flexibility.

Flexographic is a form of letterpress printing in which the impression is made from a raised rubber plate. It is used in printing transparent film and label stock for packaging and display materials.

Lithography

Lithography is printing from a flat surface, originally called planographic printing. It is based on the principle that oil and water don't mix. The ad is transferred photographically to a thin metal plate and a greasy ink is applied. Water washes the plate, except where it is repelled by the greasy ink area.

In *direct* lithography the inked plate (which is on a rotating cylinder) transfers the ad impression to paper as it is fed through the press under the cylinder. This method is highly rated for vivid color reproduction and is used on certain types of outdoor posters and large-size store displays.

The more common method of lithography is called *offset.* The principle is the same, but here the image is transferred from the plate to a rubber roller (or blanket) which, in turn, prints the paper. This is the fastest growing and most widely used form of printing for most advertising work. It is ideal for catalogs, brochures, and all literature. Every year more magazines and newspapers are converting to offset.

Intaglio (or Gravure)

Intaglio (or *gravure*) is printing from a depressed surface, as in the case of an engraved calling card. Ink flows over the plate and is retained in the etched portions. The flat surfaces are wiped clean. The plate then transfers the ink to paper in the printing process. Plate costs are high, but for long runs at fast speeds, where color is used on relatively inexpensive paper, gravure is best. Most newspaper "Sunday supplements" are printed by gravure. Also, color newspaper inserts, commonly known as "Hi-Fi ROP Color" or "SpectaColor," are produced by the gravure process.

Silkscreen

Silkscreen printing is ideal for short quantity requirements of signs, posters, displays, containers, and apparel. The printing is done through a silk, nylon, or stainless steel mesh screen drawn tight over a frame. A hand-cut or photographically prepared stencil is placed on the screen and blocks out areas not to be printed. By squeegee or roller the ink is forced through the screen onto the paper. Halftone reproduction by this process is limited to a coarse screen dot pattern (approximately 30 lines per inch, compared to 60 lines for newspapers, 120 lines for magazines, and 150 lines for brochures). At a distance the coarse screen stands up very well, but for closer viewing, posterized art techniques give better reproduction.

PHOTOENGRAVING

To print the ad by any of the printing processes except silkscreen, it is necessary to photoengrave or photogravure the artwork and type.

The first step is to make two photographs: a photograph of the mechanicals (all type matter, etc., pasted into position); and a photograph of the illustration material.

Two different types of negatives are needed: a line negative of all type including line drawings, and a halftone (dot) negative of all photographs or "tone" artwork. These are then stripped together. Solid areas or lines may be reduced in value by stripping in mechanical screens with dot patterns of varying intensity. Delicate values, especially in multicolor photoengraving, may require the engraver to make a series of internegatives and combine them to achieve the desired values.

In color printing, a separate negative is made for each color. In process printing, four colors (magenta, yellow, cyan, and black), properly separated and made into negatives, are required for full-color reproduction.

The photoengraver separates the three subtractive primary colors by means of filters and masks a specially prepared negative to obtain the black. For a full-color drawing, he uses a green filter in front of the lens to separate out and make a negative of only the blue and red values, which reproduces with magenta ink. A red filter gives him only blues and greens (cyan). And a blue filter gives him greens and reds (yellow).

When both letterpress and lithograph printing are to be done of the same color work, the production manager will save considerable money by having "Scotch-prints® " made of the letterpress plates for the lithography process.

Once the negatives are technically correct, plates may be made. The printing is done from the plates which are made by photographically transferring the image to sensitized metal. In lithography or intaglio, the image is etched into the plate. It is etched deep into the plate in the case of intaglio and very shallow (just enough to take the greasy ink) in lithography. In making the letterpress plates, the opposite is true. The design is photographically exposed on the metal in such a way that it is insoluble in acid. The engraving is then given an acid bath which etches away metal not designed to be printed. This leaves a raised image.

The halftone screens used in engraving are scaled by the number of lines, both vertical and horizontal, in a square inch. The fewer the lines, the coarser the screen or dot pattern. Which screen to use depends on the paper. The better the quality of the paper, the finer the screen that can be printed.

To help you estimate the cost of letterpress engravings, here is a list of some of the different types of plates, showing the relative cost relationships for the same size engravings. A line (or halftone) plate on zinc is the least expensive and is given an index of 1X. A halftone plate on copper is approximately twice as expensive so its index is 2X. A four-color process plate is roughly 40 times as expensive, or 40X.

The chart also shows the relative costs of comparable materials produced for use in lithography.

TYPE OF PLATE (with proofs)	LETTERPRESS COST INDEX	LITHOGRAPHY COST INDEX
1. Line	1X (zinc)	1/5X
2. Halftone	2X (copper)	1X
3. Combination (line & halftone)	3X (zinc)	1½X
4. Combination (line & halftone)	4X (copper)	2X
5. Two-color combination with Screen Tint	5½X (zinc)	5½X
6. Two-color combination with Screen Tint	8½X (copper)	5½X
7. Two-color duotone	14X (copper)	12X
8. Three-color Triple-tone	30X (copper)	20X
9. Three-color process	33X (copper)	25X
10. Four-color process	40X (copper)	29X

Duplicate plates cost about 25 percent less than originals. There are three other methods of duplicating plates at a lower cost. These are stereotypes, electrotypes, and plastic plates.

Stereotypes are made from cellulose pulp or plastic mats of the original plate. *Mats* are most commonly used to duplicate newspaper ads for multimarket schedules or as a "mat service" to dealers. This is a very inexpensive way of duplicating ads. Magazine publishers also make stereotypes of multiple page forms from molds so that original plates will not be worn by use in printing and can be used again. Original plates should be furnished the stereotyper in an unmounted form with dead metal and barriers left on the metal for shouldering the pressure during the duplicating process.

Electrotypes are made by a process similar to stereotyping. A mold is made of the plate; this is usually a special plastic compound. A shell of copper, nickel, or long-wear chromium is plated on it and is then separated. The mold may then be used again. The duplicate shell of metal is obtained electrolytically; hence the name, electrotype. The cost of electrotypes will vary little with the complexities of the original engraving. This process is ideally suited for making duplicate plates for multimagazine trade-paper schedules.

Plastic plates are made from original engravings by making a negative mold and a positive plastic duplicate. Plastic plates are less expensive than electrotypes and have a better printing quality than mats. They are used mostly in newspaper scheduling.

PAPER

Paper is another area of specialized knowledge for the production manager. Paper stock can strengthen or weaken the intended mood of a printed piece. Also, quality of reproduction can be enhanced because certain papers are made to add character to the type of material to be reproduced.

One of the key elements in planning is the *basic size* of the paper sheet. Standard size for book papers is 25 × 38 inches. For cover papers it is 20 × 26 inches. Other sizes are available. Special weights and styles of paper have their own individual dimensions. For maximum efficiency, full advantage should be taken of the paper. You should design the job to cut out economically from the standard mill sheet, as long as the *grain* of all cut-out sheets remains uniform.

Folding against the grain may require extra expense in "scoring," while folding the design *with* the grain will not. Also, most presses cannot handle sheets of cross grain without an additional "setup."

Another consideration is the *weight* of the paper; this is important in mail campaigns because of postage costs. And *opacity* must be considered in printing both sides of the sheet. There are, in fact, so many considerations here that the choice should be made with great care.

Paper stock, type, printing and engraving, packaging, display resources, suppliers, scheduling and follow-through — the production manager helps to make decisions in all of these areas.

Quality, speed, and price must always be considered in the manufacturing of any product, including an ad. Sometimes one is more important than the others. As a rule, however, the three should be in a "balanced" relationship.

A production manager must organize his time efficiently, because he handles many details, frequently against a tight schedule. Procedures for checking and double-checking to prevent errors are the order of the day. When a correction is necessary after an ad has been plated, it can be expensive and time-consuming. It is worthwhile to take the time to be thorough and accurate at each step in the production process.

CHAPTER SUMMARY

The Ad Man as a Production Manager

He directs the work that is done to make the ad.

He supervises manufacturing decisions in association with the art director.

He may also serve as purchasing agent and traffic manager.

He begins each job knowing the objective, the budget, and the deadline.

He has a sound knowledge of the components of a "print" ad and how they work together: type, printing, engraving, and paper.

8
The
ad man as a
creator of
television
commercials

The Ad Man as a Creator of Television Commercials

As the creator and producer of television commercials, you, the ad man, are trying to reach a consumer who may see more than 200 commercials a week ... 900 a month ... 10,000 a year. How do you keep him from ignoring the commercial? From daydreaming? From leaving the room to fix a snack, check on the baby, or put the dog out?

You start with a slight advantage over the publications copywriter who must induce the reader to make an unscheduled stop at his ad. In television, the viewer is already attending. Your problem is to hold his attention, to make him see, hear, and remember. Otherwise, your commercial will pass and be forgotten with the rest.

Before planning the commercial, you should know the product. You should also understand the basic sales objective; there always is one. Is the sales department primarily interested in winning new customers, holding present customers, or increasing usage of the product? Television is also used to help expand distribution, motivate salesmen, improve employee morale, or build prestige.

And you should know the prospect to whom you will be directing your commercial. You should know him almost as well as you know a friend – how he lives, what he likes, what he wants. If your commercial is to be convincing, appealing, and memorable, you will want to present it in a frame of reference that will be familiar and pleasing to the viewer. Today's viewer, moreover, is generally an experienced viewer, a connoisseur of commercials who will not accept banality, irrelevance, stridency. You want your commercial to be fresh, original, as entertaining as possible, and in good taste. All right. This sounds good on paper, but how should you go about it?

Before you reach for your big idea, consider the medium and the money involved, because you must relate your idea to the budget. Producing a television commercial may be needlessly expensive if you don't plan right.

PRODUCTION TECHNIQUES

In planning the commercial, the production technique to be used is one of the major decisions you will make. If you don't have the budget for it, you can forget *full animation*. It is the most expensive technique of all. A 58-second commercial has 1,392 video frames. Each frame requires a different "cell" of artwork, and it has to be shot "stop-motion," cell by cell.

Limited animation can reduce the cost of animation considerably. For example, a limited number of transparent cells can be used in combination with backgrounds that can be moved to give an animation effect. The shooting takes just as long, but the quantity of artwork needed is much less.

Photo animation is another device to hold costs down. Cutouts of packages in a scale of sizes can be shot in sequence on an animation stand to give the effect of movement fore and aft. This is just one illustration.

Stop-motion photography of live scenes is another TV commercial technique. It can make products appear or disappear, add type and take it out without expensive lab costs. This technique is one of your most valuable.

Live action photography is, of course, the most believable technique. It is limited only by the quality of your photography, stage setting, and models. If you can use a natural setting or small studio sets with a minimum of actors, the cost can be reasonable. It will not be reasonable if you try to produce an epic on the scale of *Cleopatra.* If this is your inclination, you'd better switch to movies and the forty-foot screen. Not only is a commercial with constant scene changes, many long shots, and a cast of thousands expensive to produce, it also is inappropriate to a screen that is less than two feet across. Television is an intimate medium; closeups give impact on the small screen, and the commercial flows smoothly with a minimum of scene changes.

Quite often, to achieve the best results within your budget, you will choose to use a combination of techniques in producing the commercial.

PLANNING THE COMMERCIAL

Time is another consideration. The average commercial lasts 58 seconds, 28 seconds, 18 seconds, or 8 seconds. The commercial should be simple, direct, and concentrated; you should be able to sum it up in one sentence. Never dilute the strength of the commercial by trying to make too many points; you will only confuse the viewer. The points that you include in the commercial should be integrated with each other and directly related to your big idea.

Be practical in your planning. If your big idea calls for a skiing scene and you know you'll be shooting the commercial in July, don't look for a ski slope, look for a new idea.

A final word in regard to the budget. Always be sure you have enough money to do quality work. You're playing in the big leagues. A ".200 hitter" leaves men on bases. The ".400 hitter" drives them home.

The big idea. You are selling a product in a short period of time on a small screen. The commercial must be built around a single big idea, dictated by the subject. You know the product; you know the viewer. What is it about the product that would be most attractive to the viewer? What can it do best for the viewer? Which of its features or benefits would he find the most desirable? You must be selective to be effective. If your big idea emphasizes the obvious, think of a new and interesting way to present it.

A "memory hook" which clings to the viewer's mind will add strength to your big idea. It may be done with words, pictures, or sound, or a combination of these elements. It gives the commercial a focal point which helps the viewer to reconstruct the commercial in his mind and to recall the sales message. It must, of course, be singular to the product, and it must be relevant. If it is irrelevant, it will steal attention from the promise rather than call attention to it.

Once you have your big idea and have summed up the commercial in one sentence, think it through visually. See it in your mind. Then write down the picture story and, opposite it, the audio track.

In TV, as in all media, you must appeal to the self-interest of the viewer. Show him how to benefit himself. Keep in mind the positioning premise and the basic copy approaches:

1. Building a personality or brand image
2. Presenting a major benefit in terms of prospects' interest
3. Stressing a unique sales feature
4. Featuring a major or minor objection converted to a sales benefit by presenting the positive side.

FORMATS

There are a variety of formats for commercials which have been proved especially effective. No matter which format is chosen, the product is always the hero of the commercial. A supporting player who steals the show may become a celebrity overnight on Broadway, but a television commercial is not theatre. A television commercial is advertising; its purpose is to sell. You are after a share of the consumer's mind. *The product is the star.*

Since TV is an entertainment and news medium, it is logical to present the commercial message within the framework of the viewer's reference, but with uniqueness. Effective formats include: (1) mood or emotion, which has the human interest values of real-life situations; (2) problem-solution, also strong on human interest; (3) humor, if it doesn't dilute the selling message and if the product is the star; (4) music; (5) news; and (6) testimonial or personality presentation.

Mood or Emotion

45-year-old widow strolls through autumn woods reflecting on husband's death and her readjustment. Woman VO: "It's been a year since John died ... thank goodness I haven't had to worry about money ... without John's insurance, I could never have made it." Annc: "This widow is an exception. A national study shows over 50% of widows were not left with enough life insurance to provide for themselves and their children ..." (Pilot Life Insurance Company)

11- and 12-year-old kids being marched into prison cells and locked in. Faces pressed against bars. Annc: "If your kid isn't getting

enough exercise ... he might as well be
locked up."
(President's Council on Physical Fitness)

This type of television commercial format
reaches the viewer by evoking a mood or an emotion.

This format must be done with care, restraint,
and good taste. If it is too obviously milking an
emotion, the viewer will reject it as unreal, ludicrous,
even embarrassing, and he will be frightened away
from the product. When done properly, however, the
viewer relates to the commercial and responds
favorably.

Problem – Solution

Terrified woman on phone to police: "help
me ... there's someone trying to break
in ... I'm alone ... " "Your address?" "8200
Norcross Road." "Ma'am ... that's in the
county ... but I'll call the Sheriff for you."
Scene freezes on terrified woman's face.
Annc: "Don't let this happen to you ... vote
for Consolidated Government ... it's bound
to be better."
(Committee for Consolidated Government)

The problem: enzyme detergents don't
remove stains ... dirt ... germs.
The solution: when you wash with enzyme
detergents, use Clorox. The commercial
presents three interviews with young women

at their washing machines. Teacher: "Clorox
removes fingerpaint stains from my
clothes ..." Housewife: "Clorox removes dirt
from my husband's work clothes ..." Young
mother: "Clorox removes germs from my
baby's diapers ..."
(Clorox Bleach)

The problem-solution format sets up a problem
and then solves it by illustration or demonstration.
The problem-solution format is a story with a happy
ending. The hero/product provides the solution to the
problem; it shows the prospect what it can do for
him.

Humor

Dashing man with mustache dons racing gear
in dramatic fashion as if he were about to
start in *Grand Prix* — goggles are adjusted,
gloves drawn over fingers with meticulous
care, scarf flung around neck. He then jumps
into that symbol of the suburbs, a new
station wagon, and drives away. Annc:
"Drive a new car soon with a Hamilton
Bank Auto Loan ..." Close with musical
theme.
(Hamilton National Bank)

Man alone at a table in restaurant, waiter
hovering in background. Camera comes in
close, and man dejectedly says, "Try

it ... you'll like it ... I tried it ... thought I
was *gonna ... die.*" Cut to product. (Fizzz in
glass.) Cut back to man, who smilingly says,
"Try it ... you'll like it."
(Alka Seltzer)

Humor is probably the most difficult format to
use. The life of most humorous commercials is limited;
they seldom enjoy a long run. A joke is funny the
first time you hear it, moderately funny the second
time, and, frequently, not at all funny the third.

Humor is for specialists. In the right hands, it
can add fun and give the viewer a friendly feeling
about the product. We tend to like a person who can
laugh at himself. In the same way, we can feel friendly
towards a product that doesn't always take itself
seriously.

Music

Setting is a park bench with single tree in
limbo. Cast is six dancers in limbo costumes.
They do a contemporary choreographic
interpretation of enjoying the park as chorus
with full instrumental background sings
modern jingle. "The Park is for people, all
kinds of people ..."
(The Park National Bank)

People of all nationalities gathered on a
hilltop in Rome singing "I'd like to buy the
world a Coke ..."
(Coca Cola)

The music format is as effective as the music is good. Writing a "hit" jingle is not easy, but when done well, it ranks high in impact and recall. It is an excellent device for audio and video interpretation of the brand name or logotype. It can add a "living quality" to a static symbol. It can identify a market, create empathy with the viewer, make a product take on an atmosphere of fun, brightness, strength, or any other desirable association. It all depends on the words, the rhythm, and the melody. Music is especially effective with children. The Lay's "Three Little Pigs" jingle was put on record and sold at a self-liquidating price with a label from the product. This offer went on for 10 years. We estimated that in Lay's marketing area, one percent of all families with children under 8 years of age listened at some time to the Lay's "jingle" commercial on their home record players. The same type of acceptance has been enjoyed by the bakers of "Little Debbie cakes and pies." The "Sail With The Pilot" march for Pilot Life Insurance Company enjoyed such acceptance that over 200 colleges, universities, and high schools added it to their repertoire.

News

Fisherman in boat ... underwater
photography of lure descending into water
and being retrieved ... still underwater, action
photography of fish striking and fighting
lure it has taken ... on top of water action
shows fisherman boating fish. VO: "The new

Doll Spin Glider has built-in action that looks like live action to a fish ... always swimming until that moment the fish strikes ... whether you're a beginner or a pro, you can catch more fish with the new Doll Spin Glider."
(Thompson Fishing Tackle Company)

"Pringle's New-Fangled Potato Chips." Announcer tells of new product introduction, and a lively jingle tells the story of chips. They are made by a special process so they are uniform in size and shape and come stacked in a canister so they are always fresh and crunchy, never broken. Video: happy family in park, action shots as family members enjoy their outing and the chips, with cuts to ECU product in and out of canister.
(Pringle's New-Fangled Potato Chips, Procter and Gamble)

An effective format is the news commercial, with news about the product featured.

The product itself may be new ... or improved ... redesigned ... had a new ingredient added. Tests may have shown that it is superior in performance to its competitors. All this is news.

Names make news in the newspapers. Facts make news in a television commercial. It is not enough for the product to be bigger or better or improved. Don't brag; be specific.

Testimonial or Personality

Roy Rogers, king of the cowboys, on location at his ranch as a side of beef is roasting on an open fire. "Folks, for a real western style roast beef sandwich with lean juicy roast beef piled high on a sesame seed bun, visit us at the Roy Rogers Family Restaurant ..."
(Roy Rogers Family Restaurants)

Edie Adams on Hollywood stage set for Muriel Cigars. "Hey, big spender ... spend a little dime with me ..."
(Consolidated Cigar Corporation)

Testimonials by real people may be a part of any commercial or a format in itself. The same is true when the delivery of the advertising message is by a name personality. Pro athletes sell razor blades. Betty Grable (now in her 50's and looking years younger) sells pharmaceuticals. Arthur Godfrey sells cars and detergents. The list is endless.

WRITING THE COMMERCIAL

The most important single thing is the idea or concept.

The *first ten seconds* of a commercial, like the first ten seconds of a personal sales call, are the most important ones. During this time, you will either gain or lose the prospect's attention and interest. Keep openings fresh, relevant, and interesting, and while you may repeat other parts of your commercial *in a series of commercials*, as a general rule do not repeat the opening.

You will do well to *state the promise at least twice.* Illustrate it pictorially. If additional emphasis is needed, print it on the screen as a "title" or "super." Words in the titles or supers *must be* identical with words that are being spoken.

Use *sound* to dramatize the promise. Sound effects are important, especially incidental sounds. They add interest; they make the pictures more believable and real; they aid recall. Sound has sales power: the sound of bacon sizzling in the frying pan if you're selling bacon, the sound of typing if you're selling a soft-touch typewriter. Sound effects may be used to great advantage at the opening of the spot to get attention. And the sound of music helps a commercial, too — appropriate music.

The *brand or package* should be identified visually in the commercial. Show the package or brand name prominently, and use the brand name as often as good taste dictates in the audio.

Whenever possible, use real people and let their voices tell the story in believable situations.

An announcer on screen can distract and be remembered even when the product is not. Choose your announcer carefully. It may be preferable if you are using an announcer for him to be heard but not seen. His voice should be likable, warm, and friendly.

Usually, the video is more important than the audio, because research indicates that people learn faster and remember longer what they have seen rather than what they have heard. Pace your copy, restricting yourself to a minimum of words. Let the picture tell the story when it can. Ideally, audio and video are coordinated. As the video tells the story in pictures, the audio should be reinforcing the story by explaining what the pictures are showing. Say and show the same thing.

Six Elements to Consider

In any commercial, there are six elements to be considered *before the camera turns.*

1. Concept and copy (already discussed).

2. Pacing. This refers to timing and flow. How long should the scenes be, and how will they flow into each other? How many scenes are needed? Will the commercial move quickly or slowly? Decisions will be related to the mood the commercial aims to convey. You should limit the number of scenes, especially in 8-second commercials. Except for a "fast-cut" video effect, the minimum amount of time for any one scene is 2½ seconds, and then only if it is simple and can communicate fast.

3. Cinematography. This is the art of making moving pictures; the actual quality of the photography. Interesting angles. Composition, as in an illustration. Lighting.

4. Sound and music. Sound is a part of the picture – it conveys the feeling of the picture as well as the picture itself. Should the sound be muted, restful? Fast-paced and loud? Again, the mood of the

commercial will dictate decisions — a mother administering a soothing cough syrup to her feverish child in the middle of the night would obviously be accompanied by violins, not trumpets.

5. Editing. Cut points for scenes should be planned before the commercial is shot. The scene must be maintained long enough to be understood. Avoid abrupt cuts. How will camera angles differ from each other in the same scene? Plan editing carefully and logically so that the commercial has a smooth flow.

6. Showmanship. Experience is needed here! This is what makes one commercial better than another. It is knowing when to break a rule. It is a feeling for detail — casting, mannerisms, stance, choice of clothing, even hair styling.

CHAPTER SUMMARY

The Ad Man as a Creator of Television Commercials

He knows the objective, the product, and the prospect.

He knows the budget; his big idea and the production technique to be used will be related to the budget.

He decides on a production technique.

He builds his commercial around a single idea dictated by the subject.

He sums up the commercial in one sentence, thinks it through visually, and writes picture story and audio track.

He makes his appeal to the consumer's self-interest.

He makes the product the hero of the commercial, no matter what copy approach and format he uses.

He relates his commercial to his viewers' lives, but strives to make it unique.

He knows these elements must be considered before the camera turns:

> Concept and copy
> Pacing
> Cinematography
> Sound and music
> Editing
> Showmanship

9
The
ad man as a
creator of
radio
commercials

The Ad Man as a Creator of Radio Commercials

Radio. A nostalgic word for those who remember the medium during its Golden Age. The galloping hoofbeats of the great horse Silver. The Shadow's sinister chuckle. "It's a bird ... it's a plane ... it's SUPERMAN!" Could a little girl from a Colorado mining town find happiness as the wife of a wealthy, titled English nobleman? Would *Black Magic* be number one on the Hit Parade again? In the evenings, families gathered around the radio to laugh at Jack Benny, Fred Allen, Bob Hope, George and Gracie. Everyone had a favorite program — the Lux Radio Theatre or One Man's Family or Inner Sanctum.

And then came television, the exciting new medium which you could see as well as hear. America switched its allegiance to the Big Eye. Listeners became viewers.

Yet radio is alive and well. There are, on the average, 3-1/2 radios per home. And an estimated 50,000,000 car radios. A family listens to radio an average of 2-1/2 hours a day. But the family no longer sits down to listen together. The teenager takes his radio to the beach. The head of the house turns on his car radio driving to and from work. The housewife listens as she goes about the house performing her daily round of domestic chores.

Radio today is a companion for mobile America. And programming has been adapted to this new era in the life of the medium. Variety shows, drama, and comedy have all but vanished. News and music are now the staples of radio programming.

Radio is the medium in which the consumer is all ears, and its only boundaries are the limits of the listener's imagination. TV commercials and print ads are there to see, but the mind of the radio listener is neither a small screen nor a page. Radio, to quote Shakespeare out of context, is "airy nothing" and it is the listener's mind which lends substance to the spoken words. With the right words, the right music, and the right sound effects, you may, if you so choose, stage a spectacle in the listener's head which would be too costly to produce on television and unsuited to the small screen anyway.

SELLING WITH SOUND

It is up to you, the creator of radio advertising, to paint the picture of your product in the consumer's mind with sound alone. How do you start? You start by remembering that advertising is a selling tool and that your job is to use it to sell your product. Your medium is radio; you will be selling with sound, and usually you will have 60, 30, or 10 seconds in which to deliver your sales talk. *Study and consider the product and the prospect.* Before you can give the prospect his reason to buy, you must know all about him and all about the product. After you have completed your research, begin to *think about the*

type of presentation that will be most effective. Shall
it be straight commercial? Should it be dramatized?
Should it be humorous? What about music? Sound
effects? A jingle? It will depend a great deal on the
product you are selling, the market you are trying to
reach, your budget, and the overall campaign
objectives.

In any commercial, you should *deliver only one
central idea.* A barrage of sales points, no matter how
compelling each one may be individually, will
overwhelm the listener and give him no time to form a
picture of your product.

THE MESSAGE

The prospect wants information. He wants to
know what the product is, what it will do for him,
and how it will do it. Can it make his life easier,
fuller, more enjoyable? Can it solve a problem for him?
What service does it offer him? Is there news about the
product which will interest him? These are things to
think about when you are reaching for your central
idea. What is the *single, most important thing that you
can say about the product?* Your knowledge of the
product and of the prospect, your experience – what
has been successful or unsuccessful in the past – and
your judgment, your sense of *fitness,* will come into
play here.

When you have selected the one big idea, *build
the commercial around it. Repeat it over and over
again, in different ways.* This is what you want the
prospect to remember, so emphasize it. And be sure to

associate the big idea closely with the product name itself. (Your big idea may be a whammy, but its power is lost if the listener doesn't link it with the name of the product.)

Radio is an intimate medium. You are not addressing a vast, faceless audience; *you are speaking to an individual on a one-to-one basis.* You are also speaking to an individual who may be doing something else while he is listening to you – homework or loading the dishwasher or switching lanes at 70 miles per hour. You have to make him hear you. He won't hear a whisper, and he'll shrink away from a shout. Use an ordinary, conversational tone, and try to follow these general rules: Always individualize the listener by calling him "you." Be friendly, but not folksy. Be authoritative, but not overbearing. Avoid radio clichés and superlatives. Be specific; offer facts. Use down-to-earth language: simple, lively words that will lodge in the listener's head. Your sales talk should be clear, concise, convincing, and memorable.

Write to the announcer's style so that the message will not sound as if it is being read. A "read" message lacks warmth and sincerity. A "spontaneous" message is personal, vital, and immediate.

The writer of radio commercials is often advised to limit the message to less than 130 words a minute. But more important than the number of words is the number of *syllables.* Paul Harvey, to be effective, uses more words than what is considered average – but he uses, for the most part, one and two syllable words. Words of few syllables take less time to pronounce and are also easier to understand. Paul Harvey speaks rapidly, but more clearly than most people, and words of few syllables are particularly suited to his unique delivery. The number of words that you employ may vary, depending on the announcer and the message. A few words with appropriate music sometimes is all that is needed.

MUSIC AND SOUND EFFECTS

What about music and sound effects? Certainly, they can add to the impact of the sales talk and can help the listener to create mental pictures. Sound effects may attract attention, add to memorability, dramatize the sales idea, or help to develop a personality for the product. Music may be used with good effect to heighten a mood or an emotion.

And what about jingles?

It is alarming to look at statistics showing that people remember so little of what they see, hear, and read. McGraw-Hill's unpublished report on memory retention is worth noting. The study showed that within two days after learning, 20% is forgotten. Within four days, 40% is forgotten; and within 30 days, 74% is forgotten.

How do you as a radio commercial writer aid retention and forestall forgetting? One way is with jingles. Whatever you may say about jingles, there's no doubt that they stick in the mind. How many *spoken* radio or TV commercials can you remember *verbatim*? Music aids recall significantly.

A good jingle can accomplish a lot. It creates a certain feeling about the product and an image for it. And it summarizes the product benefit, presenting the message in a melody that enhances the words and makes them easy to remember.

Yesterday's jingles were little more than an obvious rhyme scheme and a simple melody. They made their point through repetition and hard sell. Today's jingles are less "jingly." Often, they are fully developed with a verse and a chorus; they offer more warmth, less hard sell, and a sound that can fool you into thinking you're listening to a popular song. But all good jingles, past or present, have this in common: they're memorable. If you can't hum it — it's not a good jingle.

WRITING JINGLES

A good copywriter should have no trouble writing a good jingle. It begins with a key copy line, the line that you want the listener to remember. Coca-Cola's "It's the real thing" comes to mind as a shining example. Go no further until you're convinced that your key line is a *selling* line and that it is believable and memorable.

The next step is to select the sound. You may choose from country, folk, or rock music; jazz; show tunes; classical programmatic themes; marches; Latin rhythms; children's tunes; contemporary popular; or special effects such as yodels, chants, or electronic interest. The sound should appeal to your market and have the rhythm best suited to the ad objective and the image you want to create for the product.

Then, together, the copywriter and the composer will pick a winner from the sound category that has been selected.

Pick a winner?

Yes. In Nashville, country music capital of the world, there are some 2,000 writers who will compose some 100,000 songs in the course of a year. Of these, only a few will become hits. This gives you an idea of the odds against producing a winner. So your starting point will be with a piece of music that has been proved successful. It will give you the rhythmic pattern to which you fit your lyrics and will provide the basic structure for the melody.

After the lyrics have been written, the composer takes over. He first develops the melody which is comparable to the layout of an ad. It is the aural visualization of the lyrics. Starting with the basic structure – the winner that has been selected as a model – the composer innovates and adapts. He changes notes, he changes tempo, and soon he has created a new winner, unrecognizable from the original while still retaining its winning essence.

Next, the composer writes the harmony. This is the color of the musical ad. It organizes and enriches the melody.

Finally, the orchestration: the choice of instruments and the assignment of individual notes to them. This is like the production specifications for a print ad and will influence the final result in the same way the art director's choice of typeface, style of art or photography, and color and finish of paper influences the print ad.

In most cases, a musical jingle will be used on both radio and television. It is important that the lyric writer think visually, so that what he writes can be seen as well as heard.

IMAGE TRANSFER FOR MULTIMEDIA CAMPAIGN

In a multimedia campaign using both TV and radio, it is a good idea to plan the radio commercials so that the pictures and story presented on TV may be transferred to radio. This is called image transfer. Key sounds in TV spots are carried over to radio spots. When the consumer listens to a radio spot in which he hears the same imaginative and descriptive sounds that are used in a television commercial for the same product, he is stimulated to see in his mind the pictures that appear on the television screen. The sound tracks of the TV and radio commercials may not necessarily be identical, because each medium has its own characteristics. The theme and identity are there, however, with whatever additional words or descriptions are needed to paint the picture clearly.

CHAPTER SUMMARY

The Ad Man as a Creator of Radio Commercials

He studies the prospect, the product, and the objective.

He must paint a picture of the product in the prospect's mind with sound alone.

He delivers only one central idea in the commercial, then repeats it in different ways.

He "speaks" to the listener in simple, everyday language suited to the style of the announcer, using a maximum of 200 syllables per minute.

He may use music, sound effects, or jingle for emphasis, impact, and to aid recall.

In a multimedia campaign using TV and radio, he plans his commercial so that the pictures and story on TV may be transferred to radio.

10
The ad man as a merchandiser and sales promoter

The Ad Man as a Merchandiser and Sales Promoter

Advertising sells to the consumer; merchandising sells the advertising program to the sales force, distributors, and retailers. Sales promotion provides additional motivation for the distributor, retailer, and consumer to buy.

The ad is effective only if the product is available to the consumer at the retail store; the product must be there when the consumer wants it. A good merchandising and sales promotion scheme aims to improve distribution of the product in consumer outlets and to increase consumer buying. There is no "Berlin Wall" separating advertising and merchandising or sales promotion. In a well-planned and executed campaign, all three become one: The Campaign.

Let us consider the parts before considering the whole.

MERCHANDISING

"Merchandising" is a word that needs defining, especially as it relates to advertising. Its normal definition would be: to engage in trade, that is, in the buying and selling of goods.

"Merchandising" as it relates to advertising has three jobs to do. One, *to educate.* Two, *to motivate.* Three, *to sell.* The initial letters of these three parts spell "ems." In printing, ems are a measure of length.

In merchandising, ems give extra length to your advertising effort.

The consumer becomes familiar with the product and its benefits through advertising. Before the advertising appears, however, salesmen, distributors, and retailers should be informed. It is important to win their enthusiasm and support for the advertising program. This is the primary function of merchandising. It is the *promotion of consumer advertising to all levels of distribution of the product.* Properly handled, merchandising of the advertising can substantially increase the value of the advertising itself. Simply having a product available at retail stores is not enough. Salesmen and dealers must be well informed. Their enthusiastic support of the campaign plan is often the critical factor.

The objective then is to get active sales cooperation from salesmen (or brokers), distributors (or wholesalers), and retailers. Start by incorporating the advertising theme into the sales talk that will be used in presenting the product. Explain the thinking and philosophy behind the advertising campaign. Show samples of ads that will be appearing and make clear the details of the advertising schedule.

Equip salesmen with portfolios that include reprints of the ad. Run ads in the trade papers that tell distributors and retailers the details of your consumer advertising, and use direct mail to further inform the same audience.

In industrial advertising, the same merchandising tenet holds true, with the emphasis on educating and motivating salesmen and distributors. Frequently, their reaction is: It must be good if the company is spending money advertising it.

SALES PROMOTION

The American Marketing Association defines sales promotion as marketing activities other than personal selling, advertising, and publicity that stimulate consumer purchasing and dealer effectiveness. Given as examples are such items as: displays, shows and exhibits, demonstrations, and various nonrecurrent selling efforts.

Sales promotion includes various incentives such as price deals, contests, premiums, or samplings. The most effective sales promotion ideas include rewards for the salesmen, the distributors, and the consumers.

Generally speaking, sales promotions are most valuable for new product introductions. Too frequent use of sales promotions can tend to lessen the quality image of the product in the ultimate purchaser's mind.

In planning a sales promotion on a product, it is best to think in terms of one of the following four time-tested methods. But it is even more important to think in terms of a fresh approach. And as with the advertising approach, it must be believable.

Price deals: These are also made to distributors and retailers to effect better distribution and shelf facings for the product.

A special retail price should not be less than 15 percent off the retail price and not less than 10 cents. On a 50-cent item, 15 percent off would be 7-1/2

cents, but this is too little; the minimum should be 10
cents. The "best" percent for a specific sale will vary
with the product and the competitive factors present
in the market at the time.

A *price deal* to consumers may be a combination
offer. Gillette uses such offers all the time, e.g., blades
and razor together at a special price. Two products
may be put together in a combination sale ... one
being an established product, the other being a new
product.

Premiums, of course, are always tied to the sale
of the product. If the consumer does not purchase the
product, there can be no premium given. It can be an
outright gift for the return of the product label, but
normally the premium offer is self-liquidating. That is,
cost of the premium, plus handling and mailing cost,
will equal money received. Retail value of the
premium is normally twice what the consumer is asked
to pay. This is possible, because the advertiser buys
the premium at manufacturing cost and saves
distributor and retailer markup.

Contests: There are basically two types. One is
the contest of skill, such as writing the last line to a
limerick or completing a puzzle. The other is a contest
of chance, most commonly a sweepstakes.

In a contest of skill, labels from the product can
be required with the entry (except in several states
that have laws to the contrary).

In a contest of chance, labels cannot be required.
Usually wording allows a contestant to send in either a
label or a facsimile. This is to avoid violation of the

lottery laws. A lottery is illegal in the United States, and a contest is held to be a lottery if it requires consideration (purchase of the product) and if the award is made on the basis of chance rather than skill.

Samples: Offering product samples is also a very effective sales promotion device. They are particularly important if the product is new. Frequently, they are tied in with demonstrations in the store, but they are also offered by direct mail.

Coupons are frequently used in connection with price deals, contests, premiums, and samples. These can be distributed in the following ways:

1. by mailing to homeowners
2. door-to-door delivery
3. by including in newspaper ads or magazine ads
4. by including as a tip-in card in a magazine or newspaper
5. by including the coupon offer on the package.

Coupons are best used to stimulate the sale of established products. Tip-in cards will give the highest redemption, and the coupon in a newspaper or magazine ad will give the lowest redemption. Coupons on the package give high redemption but do not give exposure to new households, because the coupon offer is basically going to established users of the product. Door-to-door distribution of coupons, if appropriately presented, will normally yield a higher redemption than direct-mail distribution, but will be more expensive.

Merchandising and sales promotion programs are not only a vital part of many advertising campaigns, but an important part of the advertiser's personal selling activities. Such items as sales training films, sales manuals, catalogs, exhibits, demonstrations, and cooperative advertising or display allowances are part of this total program. The methods used have one objective: to help increase distribution and speed up rate of sale in the retail store.

A CASE HISTORY

The ad man has a big job to do as a merchandiser and sales promoter of the advertising campaign. Here is a case history that illustrates how some of the techniques may be used to achieve effective results:

A full-color, Hi-Fi, full-page ad was prepared for a food client and was scheduled to appear in 15 newspapers in areas where their products were distributed.

The ad featured six different food products in the client's line. It was a flavorful ad in eye-catching, mouth-watering color, displaying the products in settings evocative of summertime and relaxation.

It was anticipated that when the ad appeared the week of August 9—14, interest in the client's products would rise markedly. In order to convert interest into sales, consumer outlets had to be ready with full selections of the products.

The objective of the merchandising plan was to reach the department managers before the ad ran, to show them the ad, and to sell them on the idea of featuring a full selection of the advertised products during the week the ad would be running.

Folders incorporating preprints of the ad were made, and a meeting of the client's salesmen was called six weeks before the ad was to appear. Copies of the ad folder were given to each salesman. Copy on the folder highlighted the advertising program ... told the merchant of schedules ... on TV ... on radio ... on billboards ... and the full-color, Hi-Fi, full-page in his local newspaper.

The salesmen were told, "This ad is a selling tool for you and your customers, the department managers, and you'll want to show it to each department buyer. This type of ad outscores any other that appears in the newspapers, and it's going to move the consumers to the counter. Use this ad to get distribution on every product in the ad."

The agency had also planned an incentive program for the salesmen which added an element of fun and competition and the chance of a reward. Equally important, the *incentive program was a way of making sure that the story would be told* to the department buyers, rather than leaving it to chance.

Here is the way the incentive program was set up. Each salesman was given a tally chart on which to note distribution of the client's products in the stores he was responsible for visiting prior to the week beginning August 9. Each of the 6 products was assigned a value in points — 3 for one, 4 for another, etc. If all 6 products were placed in a store, points totaled 22. Salesmen who got 100% distribution in any store would receive a bonus of 22 points per store. At the end of the week, the points were to be totaled, and the tally chart returned. The salesman with the highest average number of points per account would receive $200; the 2nd highest, $100; the 3rd highest, $50; and the 4th, $25. And, they had four weeks in which to improve their distribution.

In addition, an incentive program was set up for the department managers. A "Double Sweepstakes" gave them an opportunity to win a portable TV set (plus $100 in cash if they had all 6 categories of products on sale the week the drawings were made).

An entry blank gave managers details of the contest. They were asked to check the products that they would have on sale during the week of August 9–14, to sign the entry blank, and to return it to the salesman. This eliminated guesswork – the manager had to sign the card to enter the sweepstakes – return of the signed card was proof that the salesman had done his job and told his story. The retailer could expect an increase in the sale of the client's products and prepare for it by stocking counters. Not only that, he could hope to be one of the lucky guys who won the sweepstakes.

The client's salesmen were also required to arrange for display of the full-color preprint sheets in each store. Thus, advertising was merchandised to the consumer. Special "product and price" feature display sheets and "tie-in" mats for local newspapers were also used. In this way, the store could have its own sales promotion coordinated with the general advertising and merchandising efforts.

Merchandising (and sales promotion) can make or break a campaign. Merchandising the advertising, in combination with the incentive program, paid off in this case. The Hi-Fi ad had paid for itself in new distribution before it even appeared!

CHAPTER SUMMARY

The Ad Man as a Merchandiser and Sales Promoter

He sells the advertising program to the sales force, distributors, and retailers, thereby increasing the value of the advertising.

His aim is to improve distribution and increase consumer buying.

As a merchandiser, he puts together programs to educate, to motivate, and to sell.

As a sales promoter, he conceives certain marketing activities to stimulate consumer purchasing and dealer effectiveness. The promotion is built around a price deal, contest, premium, or sampling program.

II
The
ad man
as a
media planner

The Ad Man as a Media Planner

A part of planning the advertising budget is making decisions about how much money is needed and how to spend it most effectively. There are many considerations.

These days the advertising budget is usually set by the "task" method. This means measuring the market in relation to advertising objectives and then determining the cost of advertising to reach the market and obtain the objectives. This determines the "task" and establishes the amount of money needed to obtain it.

Since advertising is but one part of the total marketing program, management will review the "task" budget in relation to affordability, as a percentage of current sales or as a percentage of unit cost. If the risk seems high, a decision may be made to reduce the objectives or to seek their accomplishment over a longer period of time. In which case the budget may be tailored back. Or the budget may be increased if more can be afforded and if greater objectives are realistic.

Once the budget has been set, the job of media selection and planning must be completed.

THE MEDIA

Space or time and production costs of each medium must be considered. Each has its own distinctive characteristics.

Television. A truly mass medium within selected geographical markets. Fast acting. Strong selling. Unusually high production requirements. A degree of audience selectivity. Strong dealer enthusiasm.

Magazines. A prestige medium. Audiences may be selected by demographic characteristics (reader analysis of magazines) or by geography (national editions, regional, state, or marketing zone editions).

Business Publications. A very efficient medium. Each publication has a reasonably well defined audience or market. It may be basically vertical or horizontal. A vertical market is one within an industry, that is, textiles, food, furniture, sporting goods, etc. A vertical business publication reaches buying and selling trade influences within a particular industry. Examples: *Textile World, Men's Wear, Supermarket News, Steel, Insurance Salesman, National Petroleum News, Sporting Goods Dealer.* A horizontal business publication selects its audience by job responsibility, that is, purchasing agent, traffic manager, design engineer, finance officers, etc. Examples: *Purchasing Week, Traffic World, Design News, Financial World.*

Newspapers. A news medium. Short closing dates. Flexible. Fast acting. Broad coverage of local households, retailers, and distributors.

Newspaper Supplements. A hybrid medium. Fathered by magazines and mothered by newspapers or vice versa, this medium contains some of the characteristics of both. Readership is longer lived than newspapers; quality of reproduction is quasi-magazine; coverage is newspaper markets with multimarket, mass magazine circulation characteristics.

Radio. A background medium. Most people listen to radio while doing something else: household chores, driving, reading. Each station's programming defines its audience: adult music, country music, teenage music, sports, special news, etc. Because it relies on sound alone, frequency of announcements is required. Multiple station schedules are usually desirable for coverage of a market.

Outdoor. A billboard is a giant calling card. Highly selective for coverage of a small area or complete markets. Requires brevity of copy (5 to 10 words maximum). Full color. Good for strong package or logotype identification. Self-merchandising.

Point-of-Sale. A "traffic stopper" medium. Very flexible in design, size, and color. Can utilize motion, animation, and even sound. Can feature price as well as benefits. Completes continuity of planned program. Creates impulse purchases. Tends to replace the vanishing sales clerk.

Direct Mail. A selective medium. Preselects prospects. The two most important things in direct mail are: (1) the quality of the list, and (2) the "offer" (incentive). The message, format, and timing are other important factors. May be used on a limited or very broad basis to customers, prospects, dealers, distributors, etc. Will be used to some degree in support of every advertised product or service.

The incentive is usually a gift or a price-off deal. It invariably increases response and results in a lower net cost per reply. Here in chart form is an example of how a gift offer costing $1.00 actually can lower your cost with even a minimum increase in response. Assume a mailing of 10,000 pieces.

	Replies	Cost of Mailing	Cost of Gifts to Respondents	Total Cost	Cost Per Reply
1. No Gift Offer	300 (3%)	$1,500.00	–	$1,500.00	$5.00
2. $1.00 Gift Offer	400 (4%)	$1,500.00	$400.00	$1,900.00	$4.75

PRESTRATEGY CONSIDERATIONS

Before determining media strategy, the ad man must give consideration to:

The product – Its characteristics, personality, compatibility with various media, and sales goals.

The market – The geographical location and size of the market must be considered as well as its demographic character in terms of sex, income, education, age, health, and other factors.

Distribution – The product's availability to ultimate users; its share of retail outlets and wholesalers or distributors; the adequacy of its sales force; the preferences or media attitudes of these "trade" factors.

The Advertising Copy – The sales message and its "fit" to the media.

Merchandising or Sales Promotion Strategy —
Merchandising the advertising to the trade is very
important. Which media have the most influence with
buyers? Which are most believable? If a sales promotion
is planned, which media can best carry the message
and generate interest and understanding?

The Budget (or dollars available) — It is better to do a
good job on a selected segment of the market than an
inadequate job on the entire market. It is more
wasteful to underspend than overspend. To
underspend is to invite failure. To overspend wastes
money over and above what is needed. It is a delicate
balance, and the right decision is one that requires
expertness to the highest degree.

The Media — Each medium has its own characteristics,
as has been pointed out. Each medium must be
evaluated carefully for:

1. Coverage (geographic and demographic).
2. Dominance or basic attention value available
   to advertising campaign.
3. Frequency required to achieve goals of
   market penetration.
4. Continuity values in relation to the total
   campaign.
5. Cost efficiency of the medium in reaching
   desired audience. (Discount structures within
   each medium may influence this figure, and
   also the availability of desired space or time
   positions.)

The Competitors — Consideration must be given to
how your competition spends its money. Each

medium has its own audience profile. If you are
aiming for the same audience your competition is
advertising to, you most likely will consider matching
their dollars or bettering them. If you elect to go after
a different segment of the market than your
competition is focusing on, other factors will be more
important in deciding how much to spend wisely.
Scheduling Patterns – No one technique is best for all
products. Research helps you measure attitudes before
a campaign starts. If negative attitudes must be
overcome, heavy expenditures at the beginning may be
most effective. The same is true if you are geared to
beating a competitor to market with a new idea.
Frequently, campaigns that start small and build are
most effective, particularly where there is a
distribution lag. Established products often prefer an
"even" schedule, or an "alternating" one when
stretching the dollars is important. Seasonal factors
must also be considered. Coca-Cola helped build a
year-round business for soft drinks by advertising in
winter, "Thirst Knows No Season."

For the past 60 years or more audience
measurement studies have been going on. Today there
are more studies than "roads to Rome." There is value
in what has been done and rule-of-thumb guidelines
can be drawn. Keep in mind, however, that nothing in
media analysis can produce advertising results
comparable to the quality of the ad itself. The creative
insight and execution of the ad maker is the most
important single factor. The objective is to add to
outstanding ads excellent media judgment.

MEDIA STRATEGY

Here are media factors to consider.

Size of Ads. Ads are generally proportional in readership to ad size. As ads increase in size they attract additional readers in relation to the share of audience remaining. If a half-page ad attracted 300 readers out of 1000, the same ad in full-page size would attract 300/1000 of the remaining 700 readers, a net gain of 210 more readers for a total of 510. Theoretically, it would never be possible to obtain 100 percent readership, so be leery of the man who promises you that.

Position. From the day our mothers first taught us to read nursery rhymes, we have been reading from the top of the page to the bottom. So it is just plain common sense that more people are going to read an ad at the top of the page than at the bottom.

Studies indicate no appreciable difference in readership throughout a magazine, nor any difference for right- or left-hand pages. Ads next to editorial content rate higher than ads next to other ads, however. Back-cover ads enjoy almost twice the readership of pages inside the magazine. Inside front and back covers, generally speaking, have between 25 and 35 percent greater attention value than inside pages.

Color. Color provides increased attention values proportionally equal to its increased cost. Color offers other advantages, especially where color or "appetite appeal" is an important selling point of the product.

Length of Commercials. The sales message should be the deciding factor. If it takes 60 seconds to tell the story effectively, 30-, 20-, or 10-second announcements will not do. In television, 10-second commercials cost about half of a 60-second spot. They are worth just that. In measuring coverage, "homes reached" by 10-second commercials should be discounted 50 percent. The same is true of radio.

Generally speaking, in a free economy, cost and value have a tendency to become balanced. The overpriced medium will not long keep the business. An example is summer television.

Repeat of Ads. In both print and broadcast, studies pretty clearly indicate that ads may be repeated, within limits, without any noticeable change in effectiveness. The important question is not whether the ad will "hold up" if repeated (it will), but whether the copy is worthy of being repeated. That is: could the ad be improved or are there new significant things to say?

The Product Interest Factor. Categories of products vary greatly in their basic human interest to people. With men, we know that sports and automobiles rate high, while women's fashions, food, and furniture rate low. With women, food, personal appearance products, and household ideas rate high. Sports and business rate low. Knowledge of this basic factor is important in media planning because people select what they want to read. It can have a significant influence on readership and total audience exposure. In this regard. television, because of the captive nature of its audience, may in certain situations have an advantage over print media.

MEDIA RESEARCH

The ad man will need to do his own research or fact finding to make intelligent media recommendations. What to buy is not an easy decision. *If he has 10 choices and can buy 4 of the 10, he has 6,300 alternatives.* He will need to study and review many sources of information, including:

Standard Rate & Data Service for rates, circulation (both geographical and analytical), and editorial appeal.

Nielsen or *ARB* (Audience Rating Bureau) for television homes and audience analysis.

Pulse (or other sources) for radio audience measurement.

Publishers Information Service for information on space and expenditures by advertisers in consumer magazines, farm publications, and newspaper supplements.

Media Records for linage by product categories.

Sales Management's Survey of Buying Power for important data by city, county, and metro areas relating to retail sales, population, and effective buying income (after federal taxes). Also, data on farm markets.

U. S. Census for a wide variety of information on many phases of the nation, business, commerce, economy, and trends.

And special studies such as *Simmons, Politz, or Starch* for market demographics, user profiles, and audience characteristics.

Keep in mind that the goal of the ad man as a media planner is to determine where to spend the money and how to spend it. Where to spend it is a matter of statistical analysis and intuition; it requires finding the best match of media and market for the product. How to spend the money is a matter of strategy. Geography is one consideration. Should you try to reach a national or regional audience, concentrate on only selected key markets, or "target-in" on the major potential users? Should you use print or broadcast? Or a combination? Should you hit with an impact or build gradually to a crescendo? How much should you allow for merchandising? Before you're through you will use all these approaches and maybe even invent some new ones.

CHAPTER SUMMARY

The Ad Man as a Media Planner

His job is to plan where to spend the money and how to spend it.

Before planning media strategy, he knows

The product and the prospect

The distribution

The advertising story

The merchandising or sales promotion strategy

The advertising budget

The media

The competitors

The scheduling patterns

Media factors he must consider are

Size of ads

Position on page

Page position in the book

Color

Length of commercials

"Repeat of ads"

Product interest factor

To make his recommendations, he must have good research.

His objective is to add excellent media judgment to outstanding ads.

12
The
ad man as a
public relations
practitioner

The Ad Man as a Public Relations Practitioner

For many years, public relations was suspect. It was a front put up by a business behind which that business could operate in any way it chose. It was the way a person in the public eye tricked the public into seeing him as a hero when he actually was a villain. As for the public relations practitioner, he was a smooth confidence man, adept at gulling the naive and the innocent. (In 1913, the U. S. Civil Service created a furor by advertising for, of all things, a "Publicity Expert.")

But, through the efforts of men like Ivy Lee and Edward L. Bernays who insisted upon honesty and directness, public relations has come into its own, and the scope and importance of the public-relation man's work is being recognized and appreciated. The most successful political careers and the most successful government programs are those using effective public relations and, in fact, public relations has played a vital role in every war effort and every major business success in America.

PUBLIC RELATIONS. WHAT IT IS

What, exactly, is public relations? It is not publicity, not promotion, not propaganda. These are just three of many public relations techniques. Many people, both in the public relations field and outside it, have struggled to define public relations. The results have ranged from the simple "what you do to make people like you" to the complicated sentence that runs on so long that by the time you've reached the end you've forgotten what the beginning said.

Perhaps the easiest way to approach public relations is to think of it as a blanket term that means exactly what it says. Public relations is relations with the public. In this context, the "public" is the group or groups of people whom you wish to reach with a message. Public relations methods and media are used to determine the form of the message and the way it is transmitted to the public. The object of the message: to achieve better understanding and acceptance.

If you're a movie star, the movie fans are your public.

If you're a politician, the voters are your public.

If you're a symphony orchestra, the music lovers are your public.

If you're a company, you have several publics. You're involved in employee relations, stockholder relations, customer relations, trade relations, community relations, and political (centers of influence) relations. With so many publics to reach, no wonder you need a public relations program — and a definite public relations policy.

Some companies drift along without a formulated policy. This makes it almost impossible for the public relations man to set objectives and plan and carry out an effective public relations program.

A company's public relations policy should say something like this: we want understanding and acceptance from our various publics; in order to achieve this, these are the qualities we wish to project, these are the ideas we wish to communicate. Of course, the qualities must really exist and the ideas must have substance. Public relations that is whitewash soon wears off and the company stands revealed as a hypocrite, preaching one thing while practicing another.

Ivy Lee, crusader for truth and frankness, said about public relations policy: "No public relations ... is of any value as compared, first of all, with the soundness and rightness of policy itself and, secondly, a frank and intelligent effort to expound that policy so it may be understood by anyone and everyone."[1]

COMMUNICATING MESSAGES

Whether you're a movie star or a large corporation, you have a public with whom you must communicate. But how? There are many ways. Public relations encompasses all forms of communications and exposures. These might include:

> publicity
> advertising
> speeches
> speech and article reprints

[1] Darrow, Forrestal, Cookman, *Public Relations Handbook* (Chicago: Dartnell, 1967), Foreword.

informational brochures
movies
manuals
direct mail
annual reports
newsletters
house publications
news conferences
press releases
meetings
benefits or conventions
participation in community affairs
endorsements
public service programs
contests
awards
personal appearances
free samples
grand openings
telethons
parades
unique gimmicks, gags, and stunts

One proliferating public relations practice is the designation of special days. *Standard Rate and Data* devotes a full page to listing these occasions. We have days, weeks, even months, honoring foods — everything from pickles to pizza — culminating in "National Indigestion Season" (December 29 — January 1). December 22, when we should be finishing our Christmas shopping, finds us dutifully standing in line, flashlights in hand, participating in "National

Flashlight Battery Inspection Day." February 7-11 is "National Pay Your Bills Week," followed immediately (February 13-19) by "National Crime Prevention Week." "Monogram Your Gift Month," "National Spanish Green Olive Week," "Sweetest Day," "Fight the Filthy Fly Month," and so it goes, all year long. The public relations man planning a "National Appreciate Your Electric Pencil Sharpener Week" had better hurry and get his name in the pot before all the days are taken.

PUBLISHING A MAGAZINE

One of this agency's most successful public relations programs has been carried out through the medium of a 16-page magazine, *The Codesco Communicator*, which we produce for our client Codesco, a national dental service organization. The magazine is sent, free, to all the publics Codesco wishes to reach: its dentist/customers, its stockholders, its employees, graduating dental students, and dentists serving in the Armed Forces. This represents a mailing of approximately 50,000 copies.

Described as "a magazine for the dental profession," *The Communicator* carries articles of special interest to its publics: news of the company; an 8-page insert sent only to employees in which they exchange news and get to know each other better; stories about new developments in dentistry (with emphasis on Codesco's contributions); and feature stories which describe the achievements of dentists in such fields as public service, education, and sports. We have interviewed, among others, Governor Winfield Dunn, D.D.S., the Governor of Tennessee; Gary Cuozzo, pro football player and orthodontist; and Dr. James Shaeffer, a dentist in Parker, South Dakota, and president of the 2½-million-member National Wildlife Federation.

The magazine, a unique and effective way of communicating with those to whom Codesco's marketing program is directed, has been received enthusiastically by the profession, and has been commended by the American Dental Association.

Obviously, there is no end to the variety of public relations communication methods, which may be as simple as a letter-to-the-editor, or as unusual as a whole town. Hershey, Pennsylvania, the town that chocolate built, attracts thousands of tourists each year and is, in itself, a public relations communication made of bricks, mortar — and chocolate.

PR PRACTITIONER
TRAINING AND CHARACTERISTICS

Too many people, perhaps, tend to think of the public relations man as a promoter, a press agent, a hustler. He's the guy who rounds up 150 orphans and delivers them to Glenda Glowing's Hollywood swimming pool. And then places pictures of the star splashing happily with the orphans in publications all over the country.

It is true that public relations work requires no special education, training, or examination. Anyone may appoint himself a public relations practitioner. With this lack of regulation there are, undoubtedly, some bad apples in the barrel. But on the whole, and fortunately, most who now enter the field of public relations and *succeed* are talented men who have integrity and believe in their work.

Typically, the public relations man is a trained journalist with a newspaper or magazine background. He must be able to think, speak, and write clearly and coherently.

He's creative, an idea man. His work calls for tremendous productivity, and so he has initiative and energy.

He gets along well with people. This is a "must." It is important that he enjoy a good reputation and that he be liked, respected, and trusted by clients and media people. He will be called upon to offer public relations counsel to clients. And his media contacts are a critical factor in the success of his public relations programs. He has good taste, good judgment, and good business sense. He has a complete working knowledge of the many tools of his trade: methods, resources, techniques, communications media. Above all, he has integrity. He seeks better understanding and acceptance for his clients and so he does not inflate or misrepresent; he communicates honest ideas and information.

This definition of the public relations man was formulated in 1927 by Edward L. Bernays: "A counsel on public relations directs, advises upon, and supervises those activities of his client which affect or interest the public. He interprets the client to the public and the public to his client."[1]

He counsels, he directs, he advises, he supervises. His clients rely on him. There is certainly no room in his professional life for anything but the truth – if personal fulfillment and recognition are his objectives.

THE PRACTITIONER IN THE AD AGENCY

Here he will be concerned with giving public relations counsel to clients, and with planning, executing, and evaluating public relations programs.

Who are his clients?

Almost every organized group now recognizes the necessity of having some type of public relations program. Clients come from business and industry, from local, state, and national governments. Top prospects would include manufacturers and commercial enterprises, trade, industrial, and professional associations; political candidates; public service groups and nonprofit organizations; and educational institutions.

In planning a public relations program, the first step is *research*. If the public relations man needs to collect relevant facts and data, he turns to his public relations reference library. He learns all that he can about the client's public relations profile, marketing philosophy, and product or service. He identifies the public(s) to be reached and learns all he can about it. Through surveys conducted by himself and his

[1] Bernays, Edward L., *Public Relations* (Norman: University of Oklahoma Press, 1952), p. 94.

department, or by professionals in the field, he determines the public's attitudes and opinions in regard to his client and his client's product.

With research completed, the next step is to *define the objective* or objectives of the public relations program, using research results as a guide. How great is the gap between what the public believes about the product and what the company would like the public to believe? Has the public spotted a product weakness the company has overlooked? Is there a benefit that needs more emphasis? Does the public need more information? Does a misconception about the company need correcting? Weighing the answers to these and other questions (and always bearing in mind that public relations research deals with the capricious human mind and is not infallible), the public relations practitioner settles on the objective.

He then determines how best to reach the objective by *planning the program*. What is the message, and what media and methods should be used to communicate it to the public?

Any public relations program must be planned in the public interest. The program should not glamorize, glorify, or romanticize to the extent that it ends up by promising more than the client can deliver. If it does, the program will backfire and perform not a service but a disservice — to the public, the client, and the product.

Carrying out the program is the next step. Here is where many of the public relations practitioner's qualities come into play: writing ability, creativity, initiative, productivity. Here, too, is where his contacts are all-important. The more people he knows in media (providing, of course, that he is well liked and respected) the more exposures he will be able to get for news stories, articles, and pictures.

The final step is *evaluation*. He makes periodic evaluations as the program proceeds, making changes when they seem indicated. And, in his final evaluation, he will consider the success of the program – was it total, partial, or minimal – its strengths, its weaknesses, and why it went wrong or right.

ARTICLES AND NEWS STORIES

The public relations man in the advertising agency spends much of his time conceiving and placing articles, news stories, and photographs for television and radio as well as for newspapers and magazines.

His efforts will contribute either directly to the sale of the product, or indirectly by creating a better climate for selling. A direct contribution involves a mention of the product as editorial content. This is done not with claims, promises, or puffery, but in the form of *news*.

A glance through any magazine will show this type of public relations at work. "New products department" (*Tennis*): pictures and captions describing new products for the tennis buff. "Thermasan now ready for trailers" (*Trailer Life*): an article with explanatory diagram describing Airstream's Thermasan waste destruction system. "Buyer's Guide" (*Family Circle*): a regular feature which names the products pictured editorially in the front of the book and tells where they may be purchased. "The New Soft Contact Lens" (*Field & Stream*): an article with photographs featuring Bausch & Lomb's Soflens.

There are, of course, many other ways of getting the product in the public eye. One example: giveaways on national television programs. The product may be donated, or, if it is a small item, a small fee may be paid. This may be arranged through people who specialize in placing products on shows (and who charge a handling fee) or directly, if the public relations man has a good network contact. In any case, the product receives exposure on national television for just a fraction of the cost of buying air time.

Or, the emphasis may not be directly on the product or service *per se*, but rather on an idea, concept, or attitude which will help to create a better climate for selling. An article describing one family's fun with their snowmobile may help to convince a lot of other families they would have fun with a snowmobile, too. An article on Holland, with color photographs, could help to increase tourism in that country. A profile of the president of a large corporation can help his image — and that of his company.

What makes a good story?

It should be developed in terms of reader interest. An article focused on people will have the highest readership because that's what people like to read about most — other people. News (ideas and innovations) also rates high in readership. Causes (identifying the product or service with a social cause in the public interest) rate high, too.

A public relations article may be institutional in nature, that is, dealing with the company image. It may be educational, focused on the economic benefits of the product. Or it may be political, relating the product to social causes. But the article must *never* be thinly disguised advertising. It is reader interest, not touting the product or service, that produces the most believable and effective story.

Article Ideas Inventory

It is helpful, at the outset, to make an article "ideas" inventory, a sort of brainstorming session during which the public relations man comes up with as many ideas as he can relating to the product, the objectives of the public relations program, and the message he wants to communicate to the public.

From the inventory, the public relations man selects the article idea that seems most fitted to the particular objective he has in mind. He then sells the idea to the publication whose content and readership is best suited for the content and purpose of the article. Next, he writes the article, adapting his style to the style of the publication in which it will appear. Once the article has been dispatched, he follows up to make certain the article is published. Finally, he assists in merchandising the article by getting reprints made. These are sent to anyone whom the client wishes to influence.

In the case of general news releases for widespread distribution, he uses a checking service which supplies him with clippings from all the newspapers in which the release was printed.

The following list is an actual idea inventory prepared for an art gallery.

1. Art collecting: a rich man's hobby?
2. Southern art collections and collectors.
3. Southern artists, past and present.
4. Art as an investment.
5. Art in the mountains: the story of The Carolina Gallery.
6. Conducting an art auction.
7. The art of managing an art gallery.
8. Art and interior decoration.
9. At home with art: matching art to your home.
10. Today's art and tomorrow's architecture.
11. Art for the office.
12. How to build a private art and antiques collection.
13. Masterpieces at The Carolina Gallery.
14. Reubens in Carolina.
15. Art outlook for the 70's.
16. Recognizing tomorrow's masterpieces today.
17. How to market taste: the business of selling art.
18. The art dealer as sleuth: tracking down art treasures.
19. How a gallery protects its art.
20. How to start collecting art — and why.
21. Limited edition: the booming collector's print market.
22. How art will endure space-age technology.

23. The oldest *objet d'art* at The Carolina Gallery.
24. Art and tax laws.
25. Pictures at an exhibition: The Carolina Gallery summer show.

A CASE HISTORY

Out of the Bijou and Into the Gym

The speech quoted here was made by the author and is reprinted because it may suggest something of the personal satisfaction that a public relations man can get from his work.

".... My first year as the proprietor of an advertising agency I found myself managing the local Symphony Orchestra. When I started the agency, it was not with any ambition to become the manager of a symphony orchestra, but clients were slow to find us that year and so we took on the job. In addition to planning the public relations program, my duties included everything from selling tickets to hiring guest artists.

"In those days, performances were given in the downtown Bijou Theater. Now the Bijou may, in its day, have been a jewel, but by the time the Symphony and I converged there, the gem was tarnished. The second balcony had long ago been surrendered to the mice, and the condition of the first balcony was marginal. The stage was so small the musicians complained they felt as if they were playing in a shoe box. No one even *mentioned* acoustics. The Bijou's seating capacity was 600, but the Symphony audience had never exceeded 400 (unless you wanted to count the mice listening from the second balcony).

"The objective of the Symphony's public relations program was simple: the Symphony wanted a bigger audience. It seemed to me that more people weren't going to come to the concerts until the Symphony moved out of the Bijou. But where to? The only other place it could go, investigation proved, was to the University gymnasium. Admittedly, Bach and Beethoven weren't exactly compatible with basketball goals, but by setting up chairs on the main floor, the gym could seat 4,000 people.

"I also prevailed on the Symphony to cut the cost of season tickets in half. The conductor was agreeable because he wanted more people to hear more music. The Symphony Board was more difficult to convince. Cut the cost of tickets drastically when, with the move to the gym, expenses were rising? (Also, there were some board members who felt there were only 400 people in the city capable of appreciating good music.)

"After that battle was won, we went into action with our public relations program. We wanted to win increased acceptance for the Symphony in order to bring more people to the concerts. More people would mean more income which, in turn, would mean more opportunity for the Symphony to improve its quality, expand its activities, and offer more to the community.

"We decided the Symphony's first concert in the gym should be a *free* concert. Furthermore, the

program was to be to the liking of an audience which
had had little exposure to classical music. I made the
conductor promise me that he would play nothing
more sophisticated than Tchaikovsky's *1812 Overture*.

"We then set about publicizing the Symphony
and the free concert. We placed articles in the
newspapers. We set up a bureau to send speakers all
over the city to talk to civic and social groups — and
to hand out free tickets. We'd had 20,000 tickets
printed, and we distributed them with abandon,
handing them out, mailing them out, putting them in
the stores to be given away. We also asked merchants
to put cards and banners in their windows promoting
the Symphony and the free concert.

"Of course while all this was going on, we were
also pushing to sell season tickets. We set up a contest
in the stores using retail sales personnel. The person
selling the most season tickets would win a free trip to
Bermuda. There were other prizes, too, and the ticket
sales contest was a great success. Also, because of our
massive publicity program, we were able to sell a great
many tickets through other channels (one of which,
much to her surprise, was my secretary).

"As the time for the free concert approached,
the Symphony Board and the conductor became
increasingly apprehensive. I didn't admit it to them,
but I was a little nervous myself. True, the Symphony
had had lots of publicity — but we wouldn't know
how effective it had been until the night of the
concert. It would be a tragedy if only the original
Faithful 400 showed up. On the other hand, it would

be a disaster if 20,000 ticket-holders appeared to claim 4,000 seats.

"The night of the concert I stood at the back of the gym and watched it fill up. It filled up exactly to capacity. 4,000 people.

"And, during the months that followed, more paying customers turned up for the concerts than ever before (even though the conductor, after about the third concert, broke his promise to only play familiar classics and started sneaking in some very *unfamiliar* stuff). As for season tickets, by the end of the promotion we had sold 2,200.

"The first season was a success, so we took the Symphony account for a second season. At the end of that time, I sat down and figured out how much we'd been making on the account. It came to approximately 55 cents an hour.

"That was 23 years ago. The Symphony is now well established and has left the basketball court to perform in the Civic Auditorium. As for me, I don't seem to have the time any more to manage a symphony orchestra. We've done a lot with public relations since then, but I'll never forget standing there and watching the gym fill up. There was living proof that our program had worked – 4,000 people. It was one of the happiest moments of my life – and worth every cent the agency *didn't* make."

CHAPTER SUMMARY

The Ad Man as a PR Practitioner

He is usually a trained journalist, with a newspaper or magazine background.

He must be able to think, speak, and write clearly.

He must get along well with people. Contacts are extremely important.

He must be creative. He must have initiative and energy.

Above all, he must have integrity.

In the advertising agency he gives public relations counsel to clients and plans and executes public relations programs.

The five steps in carrying out a public relations program are:

(1) Research: knowing the product, the client's marketing philosophy, and the public to be reached.

(2) Defining the objective.

(3) Planning the program: the message, the media, and the methods.

(4) Carrying out the program: contacts are important here.

(5) Evaluating the program.

In the agency, the public relations man will spend much of his time preparing and placing stories and articles.

He makes an article ideas inventory at the outset.

Emphasis may be direct, in the form of news about the product or service, or it may be indirect, an attitude, idea or concept that will help to create a better selling climate.

What makes a good story:

(1) Article focused on people.

(2) News (ideas and innovations).

(3) Causes (identifying the product or service with a social cause in the public interest).

13
The
ad man as an
advertising
manager

The Ad Man as an Advertising Manager

He's versatile. He has to be. He's a planner, organizer, coordinator, interpreter, administrator. He's something of a psychologist, salesman, public speaker, writer, marketer, purchasing agent, and even an accountant. In addition to working with the advertising agency, he has a direct line of communication with sales managers, product managers, brand managers, marketing managers, general management, top management, engineering management, manufacturing management, and finance management.

He may be known as the advertising manager. Or director of public relations. Or sales promotion manager. Or coordinator of advertising and sales promotion. His work may encompass any one or all of these functions, depending on the size of his company, of his department, and of his advertising budget. In any event, he is a man with substantial responsibility, who must play many roles and work with many people.

PREPARING AND DIRECTING THE ADVERTISING PROGRAM

This, of course, is one of the advertising manager's most important responsibilities. And to perform effectively, he must stay in close touch with the market to determine the wants and needs of the customers. When the customer is heard, the communications needs of the company and its product lines are made known.

He must also have a thorough working knowledge of the company as a whole; and he must know the needs, plans, and objectives of each department.

With this information to draw upon, he is then in the position to suggest an advertising program that fits the marketing needs of the company.

In planning and following through on the advertising program, the ad manager takes the following steps:

1. He isolates and commits to writing the major advertising objectives.
2. He makes sure that these advertising objectives are consistent with the marketing direction of the company.
3. He drafts the advertising program.
4. He sells the advertising program to his marketing director, and, in turn, to top management.
5. Once the program has been approved, he administers it: by encouraging and protecting creativity; by seeing that the work is successfully coordinated, is consistent, and presents a single image not only through the work done by the advertising agency but also that which is done in the advertising

department and, equally important, that which might be done in other departments of the company, such as the purchasing department; by reducing the number of people involved in approving the advertising to a minimum; by coordinating the advertising and sales promotion and other functions such as public relations; by supervising and coordinating other functions, such as marketing research, corporate advertising, and product news publicity.

ADMINISTERING THE ADVERTISING BUDGET

This is another major area of responsibility for the advertising manager: determining how much money should be allocated to advertising, and how the money should be spent.

He needs to know how to arrive at the total amount of the budget, the role of advertising in the company's marketing plan, and what items should be charged to advertising.

In setting the total amount of the budget, he uses one of four traditional methods: percentage of past sales, percentage of anticipated future sales, a percentage based on past and anticipated future sales, or the task method.

The percentage methods are related to the overall percentage of the product's selling price that is allocated to cover all selling costs. The overall percentage is further broken down into specific percentages – so much for office expenses, so much for salesmen's salaries, so much for advertising, etc. The percentage arrived at for advertising is then applied to sales figures, either past or anticipated (or both), to arrive at the amount of the advertising budget.

The percentage methods are based on sales *results*. The task method is a different approach, with advertising considered as a cause of sales, rather than a result. Objectives for the company are defined for the year ahead. What is to be the share of market? The volume of sales and profits? What role will advertising be called on to play in reaching these objectives, and what tasks must advertising do in order to play its role effectively? The cost of performing these tasks then becomes the advertising budget.

The role of advertising in the market plan can affect the advertising budget in a number of ways:

If a new product is being introduced, a bigger advertising budget will be required. If a product is so unique and outstanding that its special qualities are quite apparent to its market, fewer advertising dollars are required. If the profit margin is small and the sales volume large, or the profit margin large and the sales volume small, more can be spent on advertising.

The size of the budget should be in proportion to the size of the company and the size of the market to be reached. "The more advertising we do, the better sales will be" doesn't necessarily apply to a small company with small sales or to a small market.

It's not wise to pare the budget down to a shadow of itself in a period of recession. Or to go on a wild spending spree in a period of prosperity.

The size of the budget is also related to the items that are charged to it. These include: media costs, advertising production costs, administrative costs, and research costs. The advertising manager must be wary, lest his account become a catch-all ("Where should we charge it?" "Oh, just charge it to advertising.") He should establish a definite policy stating exactly what items belong in his account and make sure the policy is honored; else he may find his advertising account has developed a slow leak (or a fast one if he has to pay for the company's yacht).

The advertising manager also allocates the dollars in his budget. The allocations are to advertising objectives (the advertising functions to be carried out); to markets (here he works with the sales department); to media (this will take the biggest bite out of the budget); and to products (with the larger share going to the product or products most in favor with the market and enjoying the largest sales volume).

There should be a reserve in the budget to allow for unforeseen events: changes in business conditions, price rises, extra or unexpected needs.

Finally, the advertising manager administers the budget. Complete and meticulous records are kept of all expenditures, actual and anticipated. Periodic checks of sales results are made. If the facts indicate the figures need to be realigned, the budget may be adjusted so that the advertising program is carried forward with greater effectiveness.

Some years ago, the *Printer's Ink* magazine compiled a white-grey-black list of ad-department charges. This list, included below, is as valid today as the day it was originally published. The *white* list indicates charges that actually belong in the ad budget. The *gray* list represents those borderline charges that belong sometimes in the ad account and sometimes not — depending on circumstances and company makeup. The *black* list is a compilation of functions that are frequently assigned to advertising but shouldn't be.

WHITE LIST

SPACE:

(Paid advertising in all recognized media, including:)

Newspapers

Magazines

Business papers

Farm papers

Class journals

Car cards

Theater programs

Outdoor

Point of purchase

Novelties

Booklets

Directories

Direct advertising

Cartons and labels (for advertising purposes, such as window displays)

Catalogs

Package inserts (when used as advertising and not just as direction sheets)

House magazines to dealers or consumers

Motion pictures (including talking pictures) when used for advertising

Slides

Export advertising

Dealer helps

Reprints of advertisements used in mail or for display

Radio

Television

All other printed and lithographed material used directly for advertising purposes

ADMINISTRATION:

Salaries of advertising department executives and employees

Office supplies and fixtures used solely by advertising department

Commissions and fees to advertising agencies, special writers or advisers

Expenses incurred by salesmen when on work for advertising department

Traveling expenses of department employees engaged in departmental business

(Note: In some companies these go into a special "Administration" account)

MECHANICAL:

Artwork

Typography

Engraving

Mats

Electros

Photographs

Radio & TV production

Package design (advertising aspects only)

Etc.

MISCELLANEOUS:

Transportation of advertising material (to include postage and other carrying charges)

Fees to window display installation services

Other miscellaneous expenses connected with items on the White List

BLACK LIST

Free goods

Picnic and bazaar programs

Charitable, religious and fraternal donations

Other expenses for goodwill purposes

Cartons

Labels

Instruction sheets

Package manufacture

Press agentry

Stationery used outside advertising department

Price list

Salesmen's calling cards

Motion pictures for sales use only

House magazines going to factory employees

Bonuses to trade

Special rebates

Membership in trade associations

Entertaining customers or prospects

Annual reports

Showrooms

Demonstration stores

Sales convention expenses

Salesmen's samples (including photographs used in lieu of samples)

Welfare activities among employees

Such recreational activities as baseball teams, etc.

Sales expenses at conventions

Cost of salesmen's automobiles

Special editions which approach advertisers on goodwill basis

GRAY LIST

Samples

Demonstrations

Fairs

Canvassing

Rent

Light

Heat

Depreciation of equipment used by advertising department

Telephone and other overhead expenses, apportioned to advertising department

House magazines going to salesmen

Advertising automobiles

Premiums

Membership in associations or other oganizations devoted to advertising

Testing bureaus

Advertising portfolios for salesmen

Contributions to special advertising funds of trade
associations

Display signs on the factory or office building

Salesmen's catalogs

Research and market investigations

Advertising allowances to trade for cooperative effort

OTHER RESPONSIBILITIES

The advertising manager's job is complex and
varies with the size and structure of his company, so
there is no hard and fast list of set responsibilities.
Basically, his business is communication — of all kinds.
He is involved with the advertising agency — and with
every department in his company, for each department
has its special communication needs.

And so he has either total or partial
responsibility in marketing research; research and
development as it relates to new products and product
improvements; packaging; sales literature; customer
service; distribution (vehicle identification); sales
promotion; merchandising; public relations; employee
relations; advertising, including national, dealer, and
cooperative advertising programs; community relations;
inquiry handling.

He is frequently called upon to handle such
activities as sales contests for salesmen, dealers, and
consumers. He may build sales kits, design and build
exhibits for trade shows or traveling displays, prepare
sales bulletins, and assist in sales training. He may

prepare and handle direct mail to the trade; select, handle, and manage premium offers. He may plan sales meetings and conventions and attend trade shows. He may be asked to supervise the preparation of motion pictures or slide presentations of product lines or manufacturing capabilities.

Other activities might include handling press conferences, being responsible for product publicity, planning and overseeing special events (such as a company open house or anniversary, or a new product introduction), and participating in community activities, including the allocation of corporate funds in support of these activities.

Assisting him in these activities are personnel in his own department and the advertising agency. The agency offers him the depth of support and the objective "outside" point-of-view that are paramount to a top-flight operation.

In addition, the agency, staffed with highly creative and knowledgeable professionals experienced in all phases of advertising and marketing, provides the advertising manager with a full complement of talents to draw upon. He benefits, too, from the staff flexibility the agency offers. At times, ten experienced men may be required to get the job done; at other times, only one or two may be needed. The agency staff at his disposal contracts or expands according to his need.

The agency is also of service to the advertising manager in that, through its work for other clients in other fields, it has an exposure to new ideas and programs which can be helpful to the advertising manager in planning his company's program.

A CASE HISTORY

The Century II Pump

Each agency-client relationship is somewhat different. But in each case the relationship is structured to do the best job by providing complementary talents from both staffs who will work together for the most efficient results.

In working with the agency, the advertising manager needs to be conversant with all facets of the company operations and product lines so he can interpret correctly the interrelationship of all company departments on the whole.

As an example of how the advertising manager works with the agency and with the company to accomplish a specific objective is to tell the story of Gilbarco's Century II pump.

Gilbarco, one of our clients, is the manufacturing division of Standard Oil of New Jersey. One of their product lines is gasoline pumps which they sell throughout the United States and in some 30 foreign countries.

Several years ago, Gilbarco's marketing manager felt the company needed to increase its share of the independent oil jobber market. To do this, he felt that a new design in a gasoline pump was needed. The objective was to create a look that would be distinctive from the ESSO pump look. Research and development came up with several ideas and one was chosen. It was a design that required retooling only in the pump housing, the least expensive variable. It also offered exciting possibilities for a customized look. By using different materials, colors, and panel arrangements, the one design offered over 150 different personalizing possibilities.

The marketing objective was to substantially increase share of market on pump sales to independent oil jobbers. The design, in flexibility and esthetics, offered sales management the product with which to set about accomplishing this goal.

The advertising manager was responsible for working with every department in the company, pulling together and coordinating the program. And he called upon the advertising agency to contribute ideas, one of which was the concept for a wall chart showing 150 various materials and color combinations which could be offered to prospective buyers on an exclusive regional basis.

The engineering and manufacturing divisions were consulted to be sure that all ideas were feasible and economical. A program for developing leads through space advertising and direct mail was written. And, in consultation with the finance department, a financing program was drawn up. Striking four-color literature was prepared, with visual emphasis on the contemporary look of the pump. The literature also included technical detail on the product features. The product was named the Century II Pump, a name which reflected its contemporary image.

To launch the Century II, the advertising manager, with assistance from the agency, was responsible for putting together a sales presentation flip chart for use by the men in the field. An exhibit was designed to present the product at trade shows, and a motor bus was equipped to feature the product as a traveling display. Sales literature was prepared. A financing plan brochure was written. Ads in a selected list of trade magazines were used to introduce the product, which offered the buyer a unique advantage: a modern looking pump customized to his own color scheme and identification format. A special direct-mail program was created with the wall chart showing the various style adaptations offered free to respondents. A short movie was made and reduced to cassette cartridges for use in the field. Quotas were established for sales territories, and sales contests with awards made the product important to the men in the field. A feature article appeared in the employee house organ.

The program paid off. Gilbarco today has a healthy share of the independent oil jobbers' market, a significant increase over their position of a few years ago.

The story of Century II illustrates the scope and variety of the advertising manager's work, and the extent of his involvement both with the agency and the company, in planning, coordinating, and executing a program.

Springboard

The advertising manager's job is an all-inclusive one, so much so that he is constantly faced with the problem of giving priority to problems. But it can be a successful and rewarding career. It may even be a springboard to greater corporate responsibility. An outstanding example was Neil McElroy. He started in the advertising department of Procter and Gamble. He rose to become director and vice-president in charge of advertising, and subsequently president of the corporation. Later he served for two years as Secretary of Defense in the Eisenhower administration and then returned to Procter and Gamble as board chairman.

CHAPTER SUMMARY

The Ad Man as an Advertising Manager

He is versatile: he plans, coordinates, organizes, interprets, and administers.

His job is complex, with many areas of responsibility. He works with the advertising agency and with every department in his company.

His major areas of responsibility include:

(1) Preparing and directing the advertising program. He must be informed about the market, the company, the needs and objectives of each department. He then determines the major advertising objectives, makes sure they are consistent with the company's marketing direction, drafts the advertising program, and has it approved. He administers the advertising program: encouraging and protecting creativity; seeing that the work is successfully coordinated, is consistent, and presents a single image; and coordinating all related functions, such as public relations.

(2) Planning and administering the advertising budget. He determines how much money should be allocated to advertising and how the money should be spent. He establishes a definite policy stating what items may be charged to his advertising account and sees that it is honored. He administers the

budget; complete records are kept and
periodic checks of sales records are made,
and adjustments in the budget are made if
necessary.

**14
The
ad man
as a
businessman**

The Ad Man as a Businessman

Outsiders tend to think of advertising as a highly creative, competitive game. They fail to realize that the so-called "Ad Game" is actually a business which operates much like any other business. Unfortunately, there are also insiders – ad men – who share much the same attitude as some outsiders do. Their business is "different." Yes, it is, but only in the sense that the products they make (ad campaigns) are different from any product made by any other type of company.

If you are a good ad man with ambitions to be an even better one, the agency as a business is going to be of great interest to you. You know that the agency makes (or loses) money just as any other business does and, basically, does it in the same way. Understanding the economics of your own business will aid you immeasurably in understanding any client's business.

BUYING-PROCESSING-SELLING

How does the ad agency, or any business, make money? The answer is that money is made (or lost) in relation to the sum of the efficiency of three parts: (1) buying, (2) manufacturing or processing, and (3) selling.

How does a bank make money? First, a bank *buys* money at the lowest competitive cost by means of demand (checking) or time (savings) deposits. Its cost is the interest to be paid to savings depositors, or the service to be provided checking account depositors. Next, the bank *processes* the money at the lowest possible cost commensurate with reasonable safety and accuracy. Modern computers now enable banks to increase volume, reducing unit cost. Finally, the bank *sells* the money at the highest earnings rate within the law, considering sound banking practice and competitive conditions. Selling the money is loaning the money at interest rates higher than the bank pays on savings, or investing the money in stocks, bonds, or other securities.

How does a food processing company make money? First, the company *buys* fresh foods from the farmer at the best price it can bargain. Next, the company *processes* the food. Washes it. Cooks it. Cuts it. Grades it. Seasons it. Packages it. To reduce this cost, the company invests in new equipment that does the job faster. It uses conveyor belts to reduce handling or labor costs. Automatic equipment does the packaging. And third, the company *sells* its product at the best price the market will accept. The higher the quality, the higher the price.

How does a department store make money? It *buys* merchandise from many manufacturers at the lowest price the store can negotiate. It *processes* the merchandising through the warehouse and onto retail counters. Sales clerks are paid to help shoppers select items. Store fixtures, credit, and other services are provided as a part of the processing cost.

("Self-service" will reduce this cost.) The store *sells* at the highest price the public will accept that is consistent with the store's objectives of volume and profit margin.

How does a textile mill, a furniture manufacturer, or an industrial products manufacturer make money? First, by the efficiency with which it *buys* raw materials. Second, by the efficiency with which it manufactures or converts the raw material into the finished product. Third, by the efficiency with which the product is *sold*. Advertising is a part of this cost.

How does an advertising agency make money? The same way. By the efficiency with which it *buys* materials and services for its operations and for use in clients' campaigns. By the efficiency with which the agency *produces* campaigns. The number of hours spent in writing, layout, planning, media buying, etc. By the price at which the agency *sells* its services. Since advertising agencies generally have an established price (as much as 15 percent media commission) for the major portion of their billing, guidelines are necessary only for noncommissionable work. Since direct labor accounts for 50% of your cost, the selling price is twice the cost of direct labor plus a supervisory fee, usually a .1765 markup on the total which yields a 15 percent margin.

COST ACCOUNTING

Agency management today calls for responsible, simplified systems of cost accounting for purposes of billing, as well as for measuring the efficiency of operations. A "job ticket" system is required for noncommissionable production work, and a "total time" system is required for general agency (commissionable) work. The advent of computers has made the latter economically feasible for even the smallest agency, provided that the system is kept simple and programmed correctly. Electronic data processing (computer) time can be bought at a reasonable price. Nine hours of computer time and seventy-five hours of "card punching" time will accommodate the annual needs of most agencies doing up to ten million dollars a year in volume. This includes quarterly reports by client or activity and by employee. The cost factor and income factor may be programmed in, or may be left out and easily calculated within a few hours by management.

The daily-time diary form is the heart of the "total time" system. Each employee records time spent on client work, general agency work and nonproductive work. Computer printouts give you a complete record and analysis of time spent on each account and each activity. Additionally, you have a profile of each employee's time and activities by calendar periods.

Time-recorded costs are recorded on a job ticket. The language of the job ticket will vary depending upon how vertical the agency is (how many production services are staffed) and the information needs of its people. The job ticket is prepared in multiple forms so that everyone concerned will have a copy. Bookkeeping posts time costs (from weekly job-ticket time sheets) and materials costs (from suppliers' invoices). These costs, both time and materials, are known as *direct* costs.

Besides direct costs an agency also has *indirect* costs, which include overhead and related items. Indirect costs are recovered by the markup on direct costs in billing job tickets and by commissions earned from media.

Here is a list of both types of costs appropriate to most agency operations.

DIRECT COSTS

1. Formal research
2. Comprehensive layout or design
3. Mechanicals
4. Art and photography
5. Photo direction
6. Talent and models
7. Creative fee, when not covered by commissions
8. Publicity
9. Music
10. Production management
11. Production travel and expenses

INDIRECT COSTS

1. Rent
2. General administration
3. Corporate finances
4. Accounting
5. Media buying and scheduling

6. Client service
7. Copy and plans, where covered by commissionable income
8. Traffic
9. All secretarial and clerical
10. Employee training
11. Nonexpensed travel, telephone, postage, etc.

MANAGEMENT: PROFICIENCIES AND RESPONSIBILITIES

The ad man who aspires to management responsibilities in an agency will need to be proficient in four areas: (1) the creation of effective advertising; (2) client service and new business acquisitions; (3) the selection, training, and development of employees; and (4) the management of money.

The preceding chapters have focused primarily on areas 1 and 2. Area 3 has been touched upon in Chapter 1. In your selection of staff members, you will look for the personal qualities enumerated in that chapter as you evaluate attitude and talent. Management responsibility inevitably involves a deep concern for people. As an executive, you will give much thought to the people who work under you. You will strive to determine each person's potential and then dedicate yourself to helping each one develop that potential. *You will fit the job to the man, not the man to the job*, for the individual will work more efficiently and with more success if his particular talents and interests are recognized and encouraged. Fitting the job to the man is a readily obtainable goal in the advertising business, because the agency serves a wide variety of accounts and performs a wide variety of services.

The fourth area, management of money, requires some financial education and a lot of common sense. Here are some rules that will serve you well. (1) Don't ever spend more than you take in! (2) Pay your bills promptly and insist that your clients pay you promptly. If they don't, resign them. (3) Keep general overhead expenses down. Spending heavily for attractive and efficient office facilities is not necessary; good taste can work wonders. (4) Pay your employees well and fairly. Provide for their future security and give them incentives for the moment.

Advertising is a business, and it is also a way of life, never filed and forgotten when the office closes, but always with you. It is a way of life that frequently means long hours, a fast pace, pressure, deadlines, headaches, frustration. Advertising is not for the fainthearted, nor is it for the easily discouraged. Hard work comes first; success comes later, sometimes a long time later. Achieving excellence and winning the recognition that goes with it may take many years.

So why on earth be an ad man?

Advertising keeps you alert; there is always a new goal to be reached, a new problem to be solved. Advertising keeps you thinking — about yourself, where you've been, where you are, where you want to go — and about others, what they want and need, how to reach them. Advertising stretches you, makes you use all of your abilities — and develop new ones. The man who finds himself in advertising finds personal fulfillment. And isn't that what the game of life is all about?

CHAPTER SUMMARY

The Ad Man as a Businessman

He understands the economics of his own business; this helps him to understand the economics of any client's business.

He understands that the ad business makes money the same way any business does, through buying/manufacturing or processing/selling.

He shares in management responsibilities and is proficient in four areas:

The creation of effective advertising

Client service and new business acquisitions

The selection, training, and development of employees

The management of money.

15
Useful
information

Useful Information

TRADE NAMES, BRAND NAMES AND TRADEMARKS

A newborn infant in a hospital is designated "Baby Boy Jones." "Jones," the name of his makers, is his "trade" name. "Baby Boy" is his generic classification, since it describes the general group to which he belongs. Then his parents name him "Willoughby." This is his "brand" name. It distinguishes him from the Jones' other children and gives him an identity within his generic classification.

In the same way, a company names a product to give it a specific identity within its generic classification and to set it apart from other products in its own family. Bristol Myers (*trade name*) makes many products, including two headache compounds: *Bufferin* and *Excedrin* (*brand names*). The brand name also denotes ownership; it is given to the product by the company and is the way the company has of marking the product as its own.

Selection of a brand name is very important (see Chapter 6). It should be appropriate to the product, that is, suggestive of the use or benefit, without being descriptive. A descriptive brand name will most likely be classified as generic and cannot be registered. Another important characteristic of a good brand name is its graphic possibilities. Sometimes a *trade character*, such as *Big Boy* for the Big Boy hamburger, is created to add a visual quality to the brand name.

Brand names and trade characters may be protected from appropriation by others by federal *trademark* registration. This is how a company protects its product's identity. Some trademarks become so closely identified with the product they are used generically by the public – *Scotch tape, Celluloid, Jell-o, Bakelite* are examples.

Companies want their product names to be well known, but they don't want them so well known they become generic. DuPont lost "nylon" because public use genericized it. Xerox Corporation was so fearful of losing its *Xerox* trademark in the same way that it issued a plea to all its subsidiary and corporate employees a few years ago asking that personnel discourage the verbal, generic use of the term wherever possible.

A trademark registration is effective from the date the product is first shipped and sold in interstate commerce, even though the application for registration is filed later. A registration remains in force 20 years and is renewable for like periods. The patent office of the U.S. Department of Commerce in Washington, D.C., will send you a booklet with complete information. (A product that does not move in interstate commerce may be protected by state registration.)

A mark is registered under a classification number. For *Goods*, there are 52 different classifications. For *Services* there are 8. Food products are classification No. 42. It is possible that a registered name in this classification may also be registered by another firm in another classification — No. 32, for instance, which is furniture. The protection is basically only for the "class of goods and services." Like names which might be misleading to the public may not be registered in different classifications. A cough drop and a cigarette would be in different classifications, but they are frequently sold in the same place. If they shared the same name, the benefits of the cough drop might be associated with the cigarette.

Synoptically, the law requires that trademarks be used as follows to be valid:

1. Placed physically on the product or its container, including tags or labels attached to the product and point-of-sale pieces used in association with the product.

2. Sold or transported in interstate commerce.

Other qualifying conditions of trademarks are (1) that the trademark is not similar to another trademark in appearance, sound, or meaning if the products are in competition; (2) that it is not descriptive or misleading; (3) that it is not a common surname; (4) that it is not in poor taste or contrary to public policy; and (5) that the symbol ® is used with the registered name.

The registration may include colors, as well as the name and the style of lettering. From time to time, a trademark can and should be revised in order to stay up to date, and to present an image consistent with the times and with the modern application of the product.

CLASSIFICATION OF GOODS AND SERVICES

Class	*Goods*
1	Raw or partly prepared materials
2	Receptacles
3	Baggage, animal equipments, portfolios, and pocketbooks
4	Abrasives and polishing materials
5	Adhesives
6	Chemicals and chemical compositions
7	Cordage
8	Smokers' articles, not including tobacco products
9	Explosives, firearms, equipments, and projectiles
10	Fertilizers
11	Inks and inking materials
12	Construction materials
13	Hardware and plumbing and steam-fitting supplies
14	Metals and metal castings and forgings
15	Oils and greases
16	Protective and decorative coatings
17	Tobacco products
18	Medicines and pharmaceutical preparations
19	Vehicles
20	Linoleum and oiled cloth
21	Electrical apparatus, machines, and supplies

22   Games, toys, and sporting goods
23   Cutlery, machinery, and tools, and parts thereof
24   Laundry appliances and machines
25   Locks and safes
26   Measuring and scientific appliances
27   Horological instruments
28   Jewelry and precious-metal ware
29   Brooms, brushes, and dusters
30   Crockery, earthen ware, and porcelain
31   Filters and refrigerators
32   Furniture and upholstery
33   Glassware
34   Heating, lighting, and ventilating apparatus
35   Belting, hose, machinery packing, and nonmetallic tires
36   Musical instruments and supplies
37   Paper and stationery
38   Prints and publications
39   Clothing
40   Fancy goods, furnishings, and notions
41   Canes, parasols, and umbrellas
42   Knitted, netted, and textile fabrics, and substitutes therefor
43   Thread and yarn
44   Dental, medical, and surgical appliances
45   Soft drinks and carbonated waters
46   Foods and ingredients of foods
47   Wines
48   Malt beverages and liquors
49   Distilled alcoholic liquors
50   Merchandise not otherwise classified
51   Cosmetics and toilet preparations

CHECKLIST FOR INCREASING PRODUCT
SALES APPEAL

Advertising has no magic that is not related to the product itself. Sometimes this means changing the product. Here is a checklist of ways in which the product (or product line) may be changed or improved to give it more market appeal and advantage.

1. Use COLOR to achieve product distinction. (Blue *Cheer, Stripe* toothpaste, pink *Lustre Cream*)

2. Create a new product by COMBINING two products into one. (Putter-coaster, sausage with bacon, clock-radio, cranberry/apple juice)

3. Add a COMPANION item at a higher or lower price. (Wood-Hood Deluxe, Signature Ham, Esso Plus)

4. Use CONVENIENCE to create new appeal. (Household spray cleaner, *Brown 'n Serve* rolls, "pop-top" cans, hot cereal prepared in the bowl)

5. Use a new FLAVOR to create new appeal.
   (Peanut butter ice cream, mint cough drops, spiced beef loaf)

6. Add an INGREDIENT that will give you an extra benefit.
   (Lemon oil in *Pledge, Koratron* in clothing, automatic color TV tuning, K2$_r$ in spot cleaner)

7. Convert a NEGATIVE to a positive in the product.
   (*Volkswagen* styling, no extra ingredients in *Bayer*)

8. Find an important NEW USE for your product.
   (Hot *Dr. Pepper*, soup for sauce or gravy, *Elmer's Glue* for fine art)

9. Use SHAPE to achieve product distinction.
   (*Dove* soap, *Log Cabin* syrup, cheeses, liquor, jellies)

10. Use SIZE to achieve product differentiation.
    (*Tiparillos, Benson & Hedges 100, Reader's Digest*, "cracker-size" Bologna)

11. Offer a CHOICE of textures or processes for broader appeal.
    (Hot or mild seasoned sausage; creamed or whole kernel corn; margarine, whipped or solid; regular or diet soft drink; transistor or plug-in TV)

12. Add VARIETIES to appeal to specialized segments of the market.
    Salad dressings (Italian, French, Russian)
    Wieners (Pork and beef, all beef, meat with soy protein added)
    Pancake mix (blueberry, buckwheat, buttermilk)
    Metrecal (cookies, soup, main course, drink)

INDEX OF PERCENTAGE OF SALES
SPENT FOR ADVERTISING

As a guide to planning, this table shows the current ratios of advertising expenditures to sales for various goods and services.

BUSINESS OR INDUSTRY	HIGH	LOW
Auto dealers	3.0%	1.0%
Automotive products	3.0%	1.0%
Banks	$1,000 per million of deposits	
Building materials dealers	2.0%	0.5%
Drugs and cosmetics	40.0%	8.0%
Food products	11.0%	2.5%
Food stores	2.0%	1.0%
Furniture and home furnishings	12.0%	2.0%
General merchandise stores	5.0%	3.0%
Household products	15.0%	3.0%
Industrial products	1.5%	0.5%
Insurance companies		
Life	0.6%	0.2%
Casualty	1.0%	0.5%
Mail order	12.0%	8.0%
Meat packers	1.0%	0.5%
Personal service companies	3.5%	1.5%
Resorts and recreation	6.0%	3.0%
Restaurant chains	5.0%	1.0%
Savings and loans	$1,300 per million of deposits	
Scientific instruments	6.0%	2.0%
Sporting goods, toys	5.0%	2.0%
Television and radio stations	3.0%	1.0%

Textile mill		
Underwear	3.0%	1.0%
Outerwear	3.0%	1.0%
High fashion	5.0%	3.0%
Theaters	10.0%	5.0%
Transportation		
Motor Freight	0.6%	0.4%
Airlines	3.0%	2.0%
Bus	1.0%	0.5%
Utilities	0.5%	0.3%

INDEX OF SALES PER EMPLOYEE

If you know the number of people employed in a particular company, you can estimate the total annual sales volume of that company. As a general rule, industries that require "hand operations" have a lower sales volume per employee than industries that are highly automated.

Vertical industries (those that start the manufacturing process with raw materials and sell a finished product) will usually have lower sales per employee than horizontal companies (those that buy component parts and fabricate or assemble the finished product).

New developments in automation have a tendency to increase sales per employee annually. Inflation has the same effect.

Industry averages of annual sales per employee can be multiplied by average advertising expenditures for the same industry to provide a rule-of-thumb index in planning the advertising budget.

Business or Industry	Sales per Employee
Auto dealers	$70,000
Automotive products	35,000
Building materials dealers	45,000
Chemical manufacturing	30,000
Drugs and cosmetics	40,000
Food products	40,000
Food stores	50,000
Furniture and home furnishings	30,000
General merchandise stores	30,000
Household products	25,000
Industrial products	25,000
Meat packers	100,000
Metal (heavy) manufacturing	30,000
Metal products	25,000
Motor vehicles	25,000
Personal service companies	18,000
Petroleum refining	70,000
Pharmaceutical manufacturing	25,000
Resorts and recreation	25,000
Restaurants	15,000
Scientific instruments	27,000
Sporting goods, toys (manufacturing)	25,000
Textile mills	20,000
Transportation	20,000

THE FUNCTIONS OF ADVERTISING

The ultimate function of advertising is sales. Most sales, however, are not immediate, even in personal selling. Study how a commission salesman cultivates his territory. He plans his work so that he will make a certain number of calls on old or existing customers and a certain number of calls on prospects each day or each week.

Advertising should work the same way. It should help keep present customers sold, while at the same time helping to sell new customers on a planned systematic basis. For this reason, the result of much advertising is long-term.

The conversion of prospects to customers through advertising follows an orderly progression. Advertising works simultaneously on a number of prospects who may have quite different attitudes toward the product or service. In order of difficulty, here are the attitudes you may encounter among prospects.

1. A negative attitude toward the product resulting from a personal experience
2. A negative attitude toward the product resulting from some communications source
3. An unawareness of the existence of the product
4. Awareness but no knowledge of the product
5. General knowledge of what the product offers
6. Approval of the product
7. Preference for the product
8. Conviction that purchase would be wise
9. Actual purchase of the product

Obviously, it will take more advertising and the longest time to convert prospects in category 1. Somewhat less in category 2, etc.

Each situation can differ. Distances between categories are not necessarily uniform. It can take weeks or months to move from category 2 to 6 and only a very short time to move from 6 to 9. The greater the economic commitment or psychological barrier involved, the longer the time needed to move the prospect up to category 9 (purchase). Conversely, the lower the price, without any change in habit or custom, the shorter the time required.

Small-priced package goods can sometimes be sold quickly through advertising, while higher priced consumer goods and industrial products require extensive education and conviction before the advertising results in a sale.

PUBLICATION ADVERTISING
TO CUT SELLING COSTS

Several years ago, McGraw-Hill published results of a survey which showed how the average industrial products salesman spends his time during a working day. The results:

Traveling and waiting — 32% of his time

Paperwork — 19% of his time

Service calls — 7% of his time

Face-to-face selling — 42% of his time

100%

Suppose a salesman's annual income (including expenses) is $15,000, and he makes sales calls an average of 200 days a year. His time is then worth $75 per day. If 42% of his time is spent in face-to-face selling, this means that the cost of a sales call amounts to $31.50 per call, no insignificant sum. Business publication advertising can help to get more mileage out of the dollars spent on sales calls by conditioning the prospect, creating awareness of the product and its advantages, and thereby increasing the salesman's efficiency in closing the sale.

Also, it maintains a contact with accounts in the territory that the salesman may not have time to see or will miss for a number of legitimate reasons. Calls in response to inquiries produced from business publication advertising have a much higher conversion rate to sales than noninquiry calls.

Studies also indicate that advertising helps to keep the customer sold, and that industrial buyers take pride in reading about companies with whom they do business.

PRICING THE PRODUCT

In recommending marketing strategy, consideration must be given to established costs of distribution, wholesale and retail. Pricing should normally follow the custom of the trade. This is another influence on advertising strategy. A representative list of established costs follows. *Markups* are figured on cost to yield like dollar-and-cent *margins* on selling price. For example, if the manufacturer's cost is $1.00, a 50% markup brings the price to $1.50. This is a 33.33% margin on selling price.

Stores	*Markup*	*Margin*
Apparel	66.67%	40%
Department	66.67%	40%
Drug	50%	33.33%
Furniture	100%	50%
Gift	66.67%	40%
Grocery	25%	20%
Hardware	66.67%	40%

Products	*Markup*	*Margin*
Apparel	66.67%	40%
Appliances	30%	23%
Autos	25%	20%
Auto accessories	50%	33.33%
Bedding	66.67%	40%
Building materials	33.33%	25%
Carpets	66.67%	40%
Ethical drugs	50%	33.33%
Food products	25%	20%
Furniture	100%	50%
Gift merchandise	66.67%	40%
Jewelry	100%	50%
Meat products	30%	23%
Proprietary drugs	30%	23%
Sporting goods	66.67%	40%

Wholesalers	*Markup*	*Margin*
Automotive	40%	28.50%
Drug	20%	16.67%
Dry goods	25%	20%
Gift distributors	50%	33.33%
Grocery (volume items)	4%	3.85%

Grocery (specialties)	20%	16.67%
Hardware	25%	20%
Rack jobbers (specialties)	33.33%	25%
Rack jobbers (staples)	20%	16.67%
Advertising agencies	17.65%	15%

COMMONLY USED PROOFREADERS' MARKS

The symbols shown below are accepted and used in composing rooms all over the world. Make a practice of using them accurately when you are making changes in your proofs. The printer will have no doubt about what you mean.

ℐ	Take out character indicated
∧	Left out, insert
#	Insert space
☉	Turn inverted letter
X	Broken letter
⊥	Push down space
eq #	Even space
⌣	Less space
⌒	Close up; no space
tr	Transpose
wf	Wrong font
lc	Lower case

sc	Small capitals
c&sc	Capital and small capitals
caps	Capitals
≡	Capitalize (used under letter)
——	Italic (used under word)
rom	Roman
∿∿	Bold face (used under word)
·········	Let it stand (used under)
sp	Spell out
¶	Start paragraph
no ¶	No paragraph; run-in
⌐¬	Raise copy
∟⌐	Lower copy
⊏	Move left
⊐	Move right
‖	Align type
=	Straighten line
⊙	Insert period
ʾ/	Insert comma
:/	Insert colon

;/	Insert semicolon
$\vee$	Insert apostrophe
$\vee \vee$	Insert quotation marks
$\overline{\wedge}$ or $-/$	Insert hyphen
$\wedge$2$\wedge$	Insert subscript figure
$\vee$2$\vee$	Insert superscript figure
?	Query for author
[/]	Insert brackets
(/)	Insert parentheses
$\mid \frac{1}{n} \mid$	Insert 1-en dash
$\mid \frac{1}{} \mid$	Insert 1-em dash
$\mid \frac{2}{} \mid$	Insert 2-em dash
□	Indent 1-em
▢▢	Indent 2-ems
▢▢▢	Indent 3-ems
ld >	Insert lead between lines
hr #	Insert hair space
⌒ℓ	Delete and close up
] [	Center copy

16
Ads at work

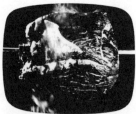

For beef eaters who like
fresh cooked meat . . .

add a barbecue sauce . . .

and you have Lay's Sloppy
Joes.

Just add water, heat,
and serve. On buns . . .

Over spaghetti or rice . . .

In a casserole . . .
Quick, convenient, and very
economical . . .

Lay's Sloppy Joes . . .
barbecue sauce and fresh
cooked beef.

A conversation with housewives. Thirty-second TV commercial answers two questions research shows housewives want answers to: What's in it? How do I serve it?

THE DAY ALBERT LEFT.

"It really hurt, losing Albert. He was a key man in our company. We begged him to stay. Even old Moody fell on his knees."

Key man insurance from Pilot could have helped to save the day. A life insurance policy for the key man, which the company owns. It offers additional financial protection for the man's family—at no cost to him. If he should die, the proceeds from the policy (tax free) come to the company which can then pay the same amount to his family as a tax-deductible business expense. And the tax saving provides funds for the company to find and train his replacement.

If they'd offered Albert the benefits of key man insurance, he probably would have stayed.

If you'd like to know how Pilot life insurance can work for your company and your key man, talk to your Pilot representative. He helps you through life.

PILOT LIFE INSURANCE COMPANY HOME OFFICE GREENSBORO N C
IN THE TOP 3% OF THE WORLD'S LEADING LIFE INSURERS
LIFE GROUP HEALTH SCHOLASTIC PENSIONS

A national magazine ad illustrates how advertising is used to position an insurance company as a resource for advanced underwriting programs.

HIGH HAMPTON

Not everyone will like it.

Over the years, we've found that not everyone
likes it here. Those that don't usually want more
plush accommodations. Ours are plain and rustic.
But, fortunately, many people do like it and come
back season after season. They come for the
unequaled scenery and complete facilities. They
come to meet other people and for peace of
mind. They come to enjoy themselves at a very
uncommercial yet distinguished resort. There's a
private 18-hole (par 71) golf course with bent
grass greens. There are 7 fast-drying tennis
courts. Three lakes (stocked with bass and trout).
Boating, swimming, riding, trap and skeet
shooting, and other sports. There's a children's
program. And 2300 acres at 3600 feet to explore.
Over 150 species of birds have been counted.
We open early May with the dogwoods in bloom,
and close late October before the majestic
autumnal colors turn to nakedness.
For brochure and rates.
**High Hampton Inn & Country Club
Cashiers, N.C. 28717. Dept. P
Phone (704)743-2411**

*A negative theme, if handled properly, can produce positive results. This
small space ad, seen in twenty magazines, pulled a record number of
inquiries. (And the provocative "Not everyone will like it" theme has
been much copied in recent years.)*

Good as gold*

*Extra hard gold

AccuMetric® System for Dentillium® CB

The AccuMetric System for Dentillium CB is a proven technique with precise controls. It consistently produces excellent restorations.

Dentillium CB is a major non-precious dental casting alloy development for fixed dental prostheses. It has all of the mechanical and physical characteristics of an extra hard type gold alloy.

Special advantages for the dental laboratory.

Great strength. Dentillium CB restorations can be thinner and more delicate than those prepared from gold.

Hardness. Similar to extra hard gold alloys, but less than that of natural tooth enamel.

Burnishability. Dentillium CB is readily burnishable.

Lightweight. The specific gravity of Dentillium CB is less than half that of gold;

restorations are therefore lighter.

Labor costs. Minimum time is required to fit the cast.

A non-precious alloy. Fixed price quotations and estimates can be offered to customers.

For professional literature, write: Codesco Products Division, 460 North Sixth Street, Philadelphia, Pennsylvania 19123

Business publication ad illustrates marketing strategy of positioning Dentillium CB against gold (rather than against other non-precious dental alloys) for a specialized share of the market.

The 15-year gamble

Maybe he'll get a scholarship. Maybe he won't.

Based on last year's high school graduating class he's got one chance in one hundred.

And you don't have to be a gambler to understand those odds.

But it is a gamble—and not a very good one if you wait fifteen years to find out.

Just $5.00 a week in an Education Savings Account at PS&L will give you over $5,000.00 in fifteen years. And that's no gamble.

You might even call it a sure thing.

Peoples Savings and Loan Association, Fourth & Market Streets, 4709 Oleander Dr., Wilmington, N.C. **ps&l**

The original "Save With A Purpose" concept shown here (this newspaper ad is an example) has won wide acceptance and has been used by many agencies, banks, and financial institutions.

WELLINGTON GALLERIES

Sale

NOW THROUGH SATURDAY.

Prices are reduced up to 75% and more.

This is a Sale. Is this a Sale. It's our big one, not just for this year, but for any year we've been in business.

We've put everything we have into it. Literally.

The things we've been stocking up on heavily—furnishings that seemed to be the most popular in past sales.

The things we bought at last month's Home Furnishings Show in High Point.

And all merchandise we already had on hand. Every bit of it.

You know all our names: Drexel, Founders, Heritage, Henredon and Selig. Medallion, Brandt, Kay-Lyn, Directional and Lane.

Tomlinson, Thayer Coggin, Hickory Chair and Woodmark. And Baker, Thomasville, Century and Craft Associates. And more.

You see why our sale is lasting a whole week. It's the first time we've gone on so long. Or come on so strong.

Yes, we've put everything we have into this sale.

And you can take anything you want out of it.

Wellington Galleries

7200 Kingston Pike, NW

Dramatic, sophisticated type handling in this full-page newspaper ad generates "sale" excitement and, at the same time, maintains the store's quality image.

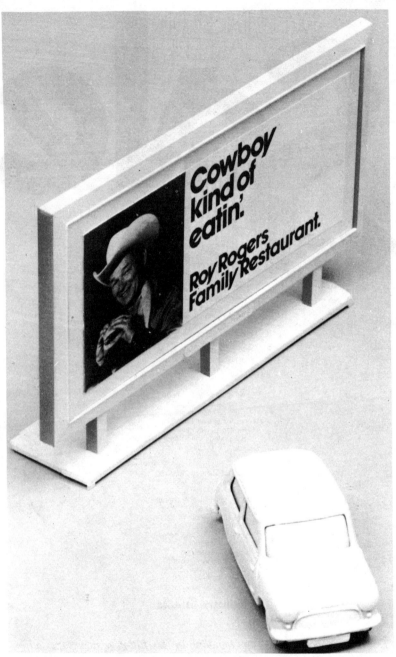

An outdoor poster design that communicates through full color, a name personality, and short copy.

Direct mail pre-selects its audience. An action format includes letter, folder, offer, and postage free reply card and envelope.

The Mason and Dixon Lines, Inc.
Visual Identification Manual

General Offices
P.O. Box 969
Kingsport, Tennessee
37662
(615) 246-4121

The Mason and Dixon Lines, Inc.

The Mason and Dixon Lines, Inc.
General Offices
P.O. Box 969
Kingsport, Tennessee
37662

Richard J. Payton
Director - Sales

The Mason and Dixon Lines, Inc.
General Offices
P.O. Box 969
Kingsport, Tennessee
37662
(615) 246-4121

Mason Dixon

A contemporary corporate identity program coordinates design of stationery, equipment, and all visual media.

Strong graphics and visual interest — especially full color photography — are important to literature and catalog design.

Annual reports can be as imaginative as other advertising messages, as illustrated by this unique front and back cover treatment.

**17
A picture
tour
through
an advertising
agency**

A LOOK AT AN ADVERTISING AGENCY. *(A) A building especially designed for agency work and staffed by many talented people. (B) Planning session, where the campaign starts. (C) Market and media planning target the audience and allocate the budget. (D) Research helps to provide direction. Data processing of information may be used.*

(E) Creative involves the marriage of copy and design. Decide first what to say, then how to say it. (F) The designer at work. (G) The art department executes the concepts. (H) The print media work is reviewed.

(I) Illustration photographs and television commercials are produced. (J) Camera, lights, action. (K) Sound track for broadcast is recorded. (L) The public relations department handles publicity and events to support the campaign. (M) The accounting department checks the statements against proofs of insertions from media. Provides audit service for client.

18
Questions
and
answers

Questions and Answers

4. The marketing concept has seven component parts. Name at least five of them.

5. List four of the nine basic functions (or uses) of marketing research in the advertising agency responsibility.

6. What are the four types of marketing research done by the agency?

7. Give a brief description of each type.

8. What is the end result of marketing research in the agency responsibility?

9. Marketing research does not make _____ ; it provides _____ which lights the way.

CHAPTER THREE: THE AD MAN AS AN ACCOUNT EXECUTIVE

1. From the account executive's point of view, what is the ad business all about?

2. List the account executive's general duties.

3. What is the first ability to look for in selecting a man for account executive duties?

4. What is the second ability?

5. What is the third ability an account executive must have?

6. How can he develop this ability?

7. What is the fourth ability?

8. Why is it important?

9. What is meant by positioning?

10. There are ten steps to be taken by the account executive in planning, organizing, and carrying out a campaign. How many can you name (in logical order)?

11. How may the account executive make better use of his time and increase his efficiency?

CHAPTER FOUR: THE AD MAN AS A SALESMAN

1. Why must the account executive be a good salesman?

2. What are the three basics to keep in mind in the buyer/seller relationship?

3. Name three reasons why business losses occur.

4. What is a staging call?

5. What are the two things you talk about when making a new business call?

6. What do you do after you have learned about the prospect's company?

7. How do you close a sale?

8. What is the most frequent mistake made in new business solicitation?

9. What is the key to really good selling?

CHAPTER FIVE: THE AD MAN AS A COPYWRITER

1. What are the three steps in the creative process?

2. What must be done before the creative process begins?

3. What is a "brand image"?

4. What is the value of market research in the conception of a campaign?

5. What is the equation for a creative concept? Explain it.

6. In deciding on format, what two presentation techniques have been proven effective? Define them.

7. In writing the ad, you strive to be contemporary and to appeal to basic human psychology. What additional factors should the ad contain? How are these factors interrelated?

8. What is the most important single element in the ad? Why?

9. What is the logical order for development of the ad copy?

10. To what does the phrase "a moving parade" refer?

CHAPTER SIX: THE AD MAN AS AN ART DIRECTOR

1. What is the objective of commercial art as opposed to fine art?

2. What are the two general functions an art director performs?

3. What knowledge must the art director have before he begins his work?

4. What is the "concept sketch"?

5. What does the concept sketch usually show?

6. What is a "rough layout"?

7. What is a "finished layout," and why is it valuable?

8. Name three of the six criteria for good corporate design.

9. What cause does the art director champion?

CHAPTER SEVEN: THE AD MAN AS A PRODUCTION MANAGER

1. What are the production manager's chief responsibilities?

2. What must he know before he can start each job?

3. What are the components of a "print" ad?

4. What are the three commonly used methods of setting type?

5. Name two of the four criteria to be used in selecting typefaces?

6. Define: *points, picas, leading.*

7. Name the four printing processes that may be used to reproduce advertising materials.

8. What two types of negatives are needed in photoengraving?

9. What type of plate is the least expensive in letterpress engraving? The most expensive?

10. Name two of the four considerations in choosing paper.

CHAPTER EIGHT: THE AD MAN AS A CREATOR OF TELEVISION COMMERCIALS

1. Why does the creator of TV commercials start with a slight advantage over the creator of print ads?

2. What must you know before you plan the commercial?

3. There are five production techniques that may be used, singly or in combination. Name three of them.

4. Which technique is the most expensive? Which is the most believable?

5. Why should close-ups and a minimum of scene changes be used?

6. What's the "big idea"?

7. What is a "memory hook"?

8. Can you name three of the five formats for commercials that have been proven effective?

9. As a rule, the video is more important than the audio. Why?

10. What are three of the six elements that must be considered before the camera turns?

CHAPTER NINE: THE AD MAN AS A CREATOR OF RADIO COMMERCIALS

1. What has happened to radio since the coming of the Big Eye?

2. In radio, the consumer is "all ears." How can this be an advantage?

3. What must you know before you can give the prospect his "reason-to-buy"?

4. What are four types of presentations used in radio commercials?

5. What criteria do you use in selecting the type of presentation?

6. What should the commercial be built around?

7. Why use words of few syllables?

8. What is the value of a good jingle?

9. What are the five steps to be taken in writing a jingle?

10. What is meant by *"image transfer"*? Why is it effective?

CHAPTER TEN: THE AD MAN AS A MERCHANDISER AND SALES PROMOTER

1. What does merchandising sell, and to whom?

2. What are the aims of a merchandising and sales promotion scheme?

3. Merchandising, as related to advertising, has three jobs to do. What are they?

4. How can merchandising the advertising increase the value of the advertising itself?

5. How does the American Marketing Association define *sales promotion*?

6. When are sales promotions generally the most effective?

7. Name three of the four time-tested methods of sales promotion.

8. What was the objective of the agency's merchandising plan for Lay's?

9. What was the purpose of the incentive program that was planned for Lay's salesmen?

10. How did "merchandising the advertising" work out in the case of the program for Lay's?

CHAPTER ELEVEN: THE AD MAN AS A MEDIA PLANNER

1. How is the advertising budget usually set?

2. Explain this method.

3. In selecting media, what costs are considered?

4. What are the chief characteristics of one of the following media: (1) Television, (2) Magazines, (3) Radio.

5. Name four of the nine factors that must be considered before determining media strategy.

6. What is the best position on the page and why?

7. What is the Product Interest Factor?

8. Name three of the sources the ad man may use in

the research and fact-finding needed for intelligent media recommendations.

9. What is the goal of the ad man as media planner?

CHAPTER TWELVE: THE AD MAN AS A PUBLIC RELATIONS PRACTITIONER

1. Name two public relations pioneers who insisted on honesty and directness in public relations.

2. What does "public" mean, in the public relations context?

3. Name 2 of the publics a company must reach.

4. Name 5 types of public relations communications or exposures.

5. Why are "contacts" so important to a public relations man's success?

6. What are 2 of the 5 steps in carrying out a public relations program?

7. What type of public relations story or article has the highest readership potential?

8. What is an "article ideas inventory"?

CHAPTER THIRTEEN: THE AD MAN AS AN ADVERTISING MANAGER

1. Name two of the advertising manager's major areas of responsibility.

2. Name two of the four traditional methods of setting the budget.

3. What is the "white, gray, and black" list?

4. Name three other areas in which the advertising manager may have responsibility.

5. Name three ways in which the advertising agency is of value to the advertising manager.

6. In the case of Gilbarco's Century II pump, what was the marketing objective?

7. Name three of the advertising manager's functions in assisting with the launching of the Century II pump.

8. Who was Neil McElroy?

CHAPTER FOURTEEN: THE AD MAN AS A BUSINESSMAN

1. If advertising isn't "the ad game," what is it?

2. What products does an advertising agency make?

3. Why is it important to understand the economics of the advertising business?

4. Money is made (or lost) in business in relation to the sum of the efficiency of three parts. What are they?

5. Explain how an advertising agency makes money.

6. What system of cost accounting is used for non-commissionable work? For commissionable work?

7. Name three direct costs in agency operation. Name three indirect costs. How are indirect costs recovered?

8. The ad man who would like management responsibility in the agency needs to be proficient in what four areas?

9. When will an individual work most efficiently and most effectively?

10. What are four common sense rules for management of money?

CHAPTER FIFTEEN: USEFUL INFORMATION

1. Explain the difference between a "trade" name and a "brand" name.

2. A company protects its product's identity by federal trademark registration. Marks are registered under classification numbers. There are _____ classifications for goods, and _____ classifications for services.

3. Name 3 of the 7 basic legal requirements for the use of a trademark.

4. Match the business or industry to the appropriate ratio of advertising expenditure to sales.

	Business or Industry		*High*	*Low*
			Ratio	
1.	Auto dealers	(a)	15%	3.0%
2.	Drugs and cosmetics	(b)	0.6%	0.2%
3.	Household products	(c)	0.5%	0.3%
4.	Mail order	(d)	3.0%	1.0%
5.	Life insurance companies	(e)	11.0%	2.5%
6.	Utilities	(f)	40.0%	8.0%
7.	Furniture	(g)	12.0%	2.0%
8.	Food products	(h)	12.0%	8.0%
9.	Industrial products	(i)	1.5%	0.5%

5. There are a number of ways in which a product's sales appeal may be increased. Match each product

listed below to the way in which its sales appeal was increased. (Use letters for your answers.)

Product

1. Peanut butter ice cream
2. Koratron in clothing
3. Hot Dr. Pepper
4. Dove soap
5. Esso Plus
6. Household spray cleaner
7. Clock-radio
8. Skim milk
9. Reader's Digest

Way of Increasing Sales Appeal

(a) Combining 2 products to make new product
(b) Companion item at higher or lower price
(c) Convenience feature
(d) New flavor
(e) Ingredient added
(f) Negative feature converted into positive
(g) New use for the product
(h) Shape for product differentiation
(i) Size for product differentiation

6. If a manufacturer's cost is $1.00 and the product sells for $1.50, how much markup does he need to apply to his cost, and what margin will it yield?

7. Furniture stores, on the average, mark up____% to yield a 50% margin on retail price.

A food product is marked up ____% to yield a 20% margin on retail price.

Automotive wholesalers mark up 40% to yield a
_____% margin on wholesale price.

An advertising agency marks up 17.65% to yield a
_____% margin on wholesale price.

8. What do the following commonly used
proofreader's marks signify?

_____

#

][

Answers

CHAPTER ONE: THE ADVERTISING AGENCY MAN

1. Advertising is a technique for selling. It is a substitute for, or an aid to, personal selling.

2. The ad man is a salesman. His job is to find out what the public wants from the product he is selling and then to offer meaningful information about it.

3. Empathy is putting yourself in the other fellow's shoes in order to understand him better. The ad man must understand his prospect in order to involve him in the selling experience and to win a favorable response from him.

4. Advertising's two primary objectives are "share of mind" and "share of market."

5. "Share of market" refers to the number of people who actually buy the product. "Share of mind" refers to the number of people who remember the message and, as a result, have some degree of preference for the product.

6. "Share of mind" is more important in the long run because it builds product acceptance and loyalty and leads eventually to greater "share of market."

7. (1) Advertising introduces the consumer to products which can make his life more comfortable and pleasant. (2) It promotes a healthier economy by moving goods, keeping employment up, prices down. (3) It largely finances entertainment and news media. (4) It increases interest in art, books, fashion, theatre, travel. (5) It calls attention to social and health problems, furthers the cause of brotherhood and worship, wins support for charitable organizations.

8. The personal qualities of the successful ad man: (1) he understands people, (2) has "know-how," (3)

initiative, (4) intellectual curiosity, (5) self-discipline, (6) awareness, (7) good taste.

CHAPTER TWO: THE AD MAN AS A MARKETING RESEARCHER

1. The marketing concept is a philosophy of business in which the company sees its product through the eyes of the consumer.

2. A company that doesn't embrace the marketing concept will lose business. It cannot reasonably hope to communicate with, and satisfy, people about whom it knows little or nothing.

3. Marketing defines the customers a company wants to serve plus learns all that can be learned about them in order to use this knowledge in the conduct of business.

4. The seven component parts of the marketing concept are (1) market research; (2) product research; (3) pricing; (4) distribution plans and policy; (5) sales objectives, budgets, and organization; (6) advertising and sales promotion; (7) selling and customer service.

5. In the advertising agency responsibility, the function of marketing research is to: (1) define advertising objectives; (2) point out problems; (3) measure attitudes; (4) define profitable markets; (5) select the right media mix; (6) select the right packaging; (7) determine the right pricing; (8) plan the merchandising; and (9) sometimes determine the right form of the product itself. *Marketing research provides information for decision-making in these areas.*

6. The four types of marketing research done by the agency are (1) *product research,* (2) *market research,* (3) *advertising research,* (4) *media research.*

7. (1) *Product research* means learning all there is to know about the product and the competitor's product. (2) *Market research* locates and characterizes markets. (3) *Advertising research* finds the most effective way of telling the story of the product to the market. (4) *Media research* helps to determine the best way of reaching the market with the ad presentation.

8. The end result of marketing research in the advertising agency responsibility is the creation of better advertising and the spending of the money in the wisest possible way.

9. Marketing research does not make *decisions*; it provides *information* which lights the way.

CHAPTER THREE: THE AD MAN AS
AN ACCOUNT EXECUTIVE

1. It is making better ads and attending to the needs of clients.

2. Some of the account executive's general duties are (1) interpreting the agency to the client, the client to the agency; (2) supervising the execution of the work done for the client; (3) preparing and placing advertising; (4) winning new clients; (5) being friend and advisor to existing clients.

3. The first ability to look for in selecting a man for account executive duties is his ability to organize.

4. The second ability centers on planning the marketing strategy, including positioning the product.

5. The third ability an account executive must have is the ability to produce ideas.

6. He can develop this habit by training himself to see everything with fresh eyes and continually asking himself "how can this be made better?"

7. The fourth ability he must have is the ability to make an effective presentation.

8. This is important because the account executive must be able to communicate ideas clearly and logically, both orally and in writing. The presentation of the advertising program is the account executive's task, and it is the presentation that gives the client his "reason to buy" the services of the agency.

9. Positioning means the unique "position" your product is communicated to achieve in the prospect's mind. It is the objective of the advertising itself.

10. These are the ten steps that an account executive takes in planning, organizing, and carrying out a campaign: (1) he defines the product; (2) he defines the market; (3) he defines the distribution; (4) he defines the objective of the campaign; (5) he is a member of the agency creative team that decides on the creative concept; (6) with the assistance of his account supervisor, he determines how much money is needed; (7) he sets up budgets and schedules; (8) he may be involved in writing and preparing the ads; (9) he plans the merchandising; (10) he manages the money.

11. The account executive may make better use of his time and increase his efficiency by making and following a plan of action in which he puts first things first.

CHAPTER FOUR: THE AD MAN AS A SALESMAN

1. The account executive must be a good salesman because it is his job to sell ideas and because management cannot be expected to recognize a good idea unless it is presented by a good salesman.

2. The three basics to keep in mind in the buyer/seller relationship are: (1) people would rather feel that they have bought something rather than that they have been sold something; (2) it is easier for people to make a series of small decisions rather than one big decision; (3) some businessmen would rather see their ideas put into effect rather than your ideas.

3. Business losses occur due to: (1) failure to attend to clients' needs; (2) failure to produce better advertising at a certain time for a specific client; (3) failure to manage the budget properly; (4) personnel changes in the client's organization; (5) the defection of an account executive to another agency, followed by the client; (6) company mergers, product obsolescence, market down-turns.

4. A staging call paves the way for selling a new idea to a client; here you review the client's problem (which you have previously "thought-out") and discuss solutions (one of which is the answer you have "thought-in").

5. When you make a new business call you talk about the prospect's business and your agency's business, *and you apply the philosophy of your business to his business.*

6. After you have learned about the prospect's company, you relate the benefits of your advertising agency service to his advertising, sales, or marketing needs.

7. You close a sale by focusing on the prospect's biggest problem and presenting a solution – your *big idea.*

8. The most frequent mistake made in new business solicitation is getting into the agency's story before it relates.

9. The key to really good selling is the service that you give after the account is yours.

CHAPTER FIVE: THE AD MAN AS A COPYWRITER

1. Three steps in the creative process are: (1) ingestion, (2) incubation, and (3) inspiration.

2. Before the creative process can begin, the problem must be properly stated and the advertising objective formulated.

3. The brand image is a picture of the product that is painted in the prospect's mind with words and visual symbols; it helps to create a personality for the product and contributes to the feeling that the prospect has about the product.

4. Market research is a valuable aid in conceiving a campaign because it helps to determine what customers want – and don't want.

5. The equation for developing a creative concept is $A + B = C$. A is our knowledge of the product in relation to the problem and the objective. B is the sum of all our other knowledge and experience. C is the creative concept, the unique but relevant way to tell the story.

6. Two presentation techniques which have been proven effective are to be "with the book" or to be "against the book." To be "with the book" means to use a format that resembles the format used for editorial content. To be "against the book" means to use a format that is strikingly different from the editorial format.

7. The ad should contain these factors: surprise, appropriateness, memorability. *Surprise* is being different – but for the ad to be *memorable* it must be obvious at once to the reader that whatever is surprising is also *appropriate* to the product, to the benefit of the product, and to the selling idea.

8. The most important single element in the ad is the headline. Eighty cents of the client's dollar goes

into the headline. The headline selects your chosen audience.

9. Logical order for development of the ad copy is this sequence: attention, interest, desire, conviction, action.

10. The phrase "a moving parade" refers to the flow of consumers coming into and leaving the market. There will always be new prospects for the product.

CHAPTER SIX: THE AD MAN AS AN ART DIRECTOR

1. Fine art expresses a personal idea or emotion. Commercial art expresses an idea about a product.

2. The art director's two general functions are to prepare the visual illustration and the layout.

3. Before he begins his work, the art director must understand the objectives of the ad; learn about the product and the prospect; know what media is to be used; understand the copy; and know what method of reproduction is to be used.

4. The "concept sketch" is the visualization of the headline idea.

5. The concept sketch will generally show one or more of the following: the product in use, the symbol of the product, the benefit of the product, the problem that the product can help solve; the market that the product serves.

6. A "rough layout" is all the elements of the ad combined: the concept sketch, headline, subheads, body copy, supplementary illustrations, logo.

7. The "finished layout" is the ad prepared to actual size. It is valuable because it shows the agency and the

client how the finished ad will look, because it is used to estimate cost, and because it serves as a blueprint for those involved in the mechanical production of the ad.

8. Some of the criteria for good corporate design are as follows: (1) the design should express the company's personality; (2) it should be esthetically and emotionally pleasing; (3) it should communicate effectively; (4) it should have integrity; (5) it should be in good taste; (6) it should be contemporary, simple, and distinctive.

9. The art director should champion the cause of the high-quality ad. He will try to sell the idea of budgeting first what it will take to produce such an ad, and *then* buying exposures in time and space with what is left over.

CHAPTER SEVEN: THE AD MAN AS A PRODUCTION MANAGER

1. The production manager's chief responsibilities are supervising manufacturing decisions and (usually) serving as purchasing agent and traffic manager.

2. Before he can start each job, the production manager must know the ad objective, the budget, and the deadline.

3. The components of a "print" ad are type, printing, engraving, paper.

4. The three commonly used methods of setting type are metal, photo composition, and pasteup.

5. The following criteria should be used in selecting typefaces: (1) the type should be easy to read, (2) it should be appropriate to the message, (3) a minimum of typefaces should be used, and (4) the type should be arranged in an orderly fashion.

6. *Points:* the measurement of type from the height of ascenders to descenders. There are 72 *points* to an inch.

Picas: the measurement of the length of type. There are six picas to an inch.

Leading: the spacing between lines of type; it is measured in points.

7. The four printing processes used in reproducing advertising materials are letterpress, lithography, gravure, silk screen.

8. The two types of negatives needed in photoengraving are the line negative (this includes type and line drawings) and the halftone negative (this includes photography and "tone" artwork).

9. The zinc plate is the least expensive in letterpress engraving. The copper four-color process plate is the most expensive.

10. In choosing paper it is important to consider: (1) the size of the sheet, (2) the grain of the sheet, (3) the weight of the sheet, and (4) the opacity of the sheet.

CHAPTER EIGHT: THE AD MAN AS A CREATOR OF TELEVISION COMMERCIALS

1. The creator of TV commercials starts with a slight advantage over the copywriter because his audience is already attending, while the print media copywriter must flag down his audience.

2. Before you can plan the commercial you must know the product, the prospect, and the sales objective.

3. Production techniques that may be used include: (1) full animation, (2) limited animation, (3) photo

animation, (4) stop-motion photography, and (5) live action photography.

4. Full animation is the most expensive technique because each frame requires a different cell of artwork and it has to be shot stop-motion, cell by cell. Live action photography is the most believable — because it's real and it's happening.

5. Closeups suit television because it is an intimate medium. A minimum of scene changes will help the commercial flow smoothly and will keep production costs down.

6. "The big idea" is the single important idea that you build the commercial around; you must decide what it is about the product that would be most appealing to the prospect. You want a single big idea because the time available is limited; for impact and memorability the commercial must not be diluted by a number of ideas.

7. A "memory hook" is a focal point in the commercial which will help the viewer reconstruct the commercial in his mind and recall the sales message. It may be done with words, pictures, sound, or a combination; but it must be relevant to the product and the promise.

8. Five formats that have been proved effective for commercials are: (1) mood or emotion, (2) problem/solution, (3) humor, (4) music, (5) news about the product.

9. The video is more important than the audio, as a rule, because people seem to learn faster and remember longer with their eyes rather than their ears. When possible, the picture should tell the story, while the audio reinforces the picture by explaining it.

10. Six elements to be considered before the camera turns are as follows: (1) concept and copy, (2) pacing,

(3) cinematography, (4) sound and music, (5) editing, (6) showmanship.

CHAPTER NINE: THE AD MAN AS A CREATOR OF RADIO COMMERCIALS

1. Since the coming of television, radio programming has changed to a news-and-music format. It no longer reaches a vast audience at a single sitting; instead, it reaches many different kinds of people in different situations at different times of day.

2. The advantage of the consumer being "all ears" is that you paint your picture with sound alone; you can create scenes and situations in his mind that would be too costly, even impossible, to produce on TV.

3. Before you can give the prospect his reason-to-buy, you must know the prospect, the product, and the sales objective.

4. These are the types of presentations: (1) straight commercial, (2) dramatized commercial, (3) humorous commercial, (4) commercial with music.

5. The type of presentation you select for your commercial will depend on the product, the market you seek to reach, the budget, and the overall campaign objectives.

6. You build the commercial around a big idea — which is the single most important thing that you can say about the product.

7. It is a good idea to use words of few syllables because they take less time to pronounce and are easy to understand.

8. A good jingle is valuable because it helps the listener to remember the product and the sales message and can help to create a "feeling" about the product.

9. In writing a jingle these are the steps to be taken: (1) select the rhythm that is best suited to the product, the sales objective, and the "feeling" you are trying to establish; (2) write the lyrics, which are copy in verse, suiting them to the rhythm you have chosen; (3) compose the melody; (4) write the harmony; (5) add the orchestration.

10. "Image transfer" is used in a multi-media campaign where both TV and radio are employed — here the radio commercials are planned so that pictures and story used on TV may be transferred to radio. Key sounds from the TV spots are carried over to the radio spots. Image transfer helps the listener to see in his mind the pictures he has seen on television.

CHAPTER TEN: THE AD MAN AS A MERCHANDISER AND SALES PROMOTER

1. Merchandising sells the advertising program to the sales force, the distributors, and the retailers.

2. The aims of a merchandising and sales promotion scheme are to improve product distribution in consumer outlets and to increase consumer buying.

3. Merchandising's three jobs, as related to advertising, are: (1) to educate, (2) to motivate, and (3) to sell.

4. Merchandising the advertising can increase the value of the advertising itself by winning the support and enthusiasm of salesmen and dealers for the advertising program. This support implements the effectiveness of the advertising.

5. The American Marketing Association defines *sales promotion* as marketing activities other than personal selling, advertising, and publicity.

6. Sales promotions are generally the most effective for new product introductions.

7. Some of the time-tested methods of sales promotion are: (1) price deals, (2) premiums, (3) contests, and (4) samples.

8. The objective of the merchandising plan for Lay's was to show Lay's distributors the Hi-Fi ad before it ran and to sell them on the idea of featuring a full selection of the advertised products during the week the ad ran — since the ad would create consumer interest, the product had to be available in the stores.

9. The purpose of the incentive program planned for the Lay's salesmen was to make sure that the story would be told to the meat market buyers. The program offered fun, competition, and the chance of a reward.

10. "Merchandising the advertising" was a great success in this case, as the Hi-Fi ad had paid for itself in new distribution before it appeared.

CHAPTER ELEVEN: THE AD MAN
AS A MEDIA PLANNER

1. The advertising budget is usually set by the "task" method.

2. The market is measured in relation to advertising objectives, and then the cost of advertising to reach the market and obtain the objectives is determined.

3. In selecting media, the costs of space or time and the production costs of each medium are considered.

4. (1) *Television* is a mass medium within selected geographical markets. It is fast acting and strong selling. Production requirements are high.

(2) Magazines are a prestige medium. Audiences are selected by demographic characteristics or by geography.

(3) *Radio* is a background medium. Listeners are doing something else as they listen. Each station defines its audience. Because message is delivered by sound alone, frequency of announcements is necessary.

5. Before determining media strategy, the following factors are considered: (1) the product, (2) the market, (3) the distribution, (4) the copy, (5) the merchandising or sales promotion strategy, (6) the budget, (7) the media, (8) the competitors, (9) scheduling patterns.

6. The top of the page is the best position simply because people read from top to bottom.

7. The Product Interest Factor means that product categories vary widely in their basic appeal. Sports and cars rate high in interest with men, low in interest with women. Fashions and foods rate high with women, low with men. It is important in media planning to be aware of this factor since people select what they want to read – thus, the factor will influence readership and total audience exposure.

8. Three sources for fact-finding and research in media planning are any of these: (1) Standard Rate and Data Service; (2) Neilsen or ARB; (3) Hooper; (4) Publishers Information Service; (5) Media Records; (6) Rorabaugh TV Spot Reports; (7) Brad-Vern Reports; (8) Sales Management's Survey of Buying Power; (9) U.S. Census; (10) Starch, Politz, or Simmons.

9. The goal of the ad man as media planner is to determine where and how to spend the money.

CHAPTER TWELVE: THE AD MAN AS A PUBLIC RELATIONS PRACTITIONER

1. Ivy Lee and Edward L. Bernays.

2. In the public relations context, "public" refers to

the specific group or groups of people whom you are trying to reach.

3. The publics a company must reach: employees, stockholders, customers (trade), customers (consumer), the community, political centers of influence.

4. Five kinds of public relations communications or exposures: publicity, advertising, speeches, speech and article reprints, informational brochures, movies, manuals, direct mail, annual reports, newsletters, house publications, news conferences, press releases, meetings, benefits, conventions, participation in community affairs, endorsements, public service programs, contests, awards, personal appearances, free samples, grand openings, telethons, parades, gimmicks, gags, and stunts.

5. "Contacts" are important to a public relations man because the more people in media who know him (and like him) the more successful he'll be in getting exposures for his clients.

6. The steps in carrying out a public relations program are: (1) research, (2) defining the objective, (3) planning the program, (4) carrying out the program, (5) evaluating the program.

7. People most like to read about people — so an article focused on people has the best potential for the highest readership.

8. An article ideas inventory is a list of all the possible story ideas for a client that the public relations man can come up with.

CHAPTER THIRTEEN: THE AD MAN AS AN ADVERTISING MANAGER

1. Two of the advertising manager's major areas of responsibility are: preparing and directing the

advertising program; planning and administering the advertising budget.

2. Two of the four traditional methods of setting the budget: (1) percentage of past sales, (2) percentage of anticipated future sales, (3) percentage based on past and anticipated future sales, (4) task method.

3. The "white, gray, and black list" is a list compiled by *Printer's Ink* to be used as a guide in deciding what charges should or should not be allocated to the advertising account.

4. Three other areas in which the advertising manager may have responsibility: marketing research, research and development, packaging, sales literature, customer service, distribution, sales promotion, merchandising, public relations, advertising (national and/or dealer or co-op programs), community relations, inquiry handling.

5. Three ways in which the advertising agency is of value to the advertising manager: depth of support, objective point-of-view, full complement of specialized talents, staff flexibility, exposure to new ideas and programs.

6. In the case of Gilbarco's Century II pump, the marketing objective was to substantially increase the share of market on pump sales to independent oil jobbers.

7. Three of the ways the advertising manager assisted in launching the Century II pump: sales presentation flip chart, trade show exhibit, traveling display, trade magazine ads, sales literature, financing plan brochure, direct mail program, movie, sales quotas and sales contest, feature article in house organ.

8. Neil McElroy is the former advertising manager for Procter & Gamble who rose to be P&G's Chairman of the Board.

CHAPTER FOURTEEN: THE AD MAN
AS A BUSINESSMAN

1. Advertising is a business and is operated as such.

2. An advertising agency makes advertising campaigns.

3. It is important for the success of an ad man's career to understand the economics of his business. Since the agency makes (or loses) money exactly as any other business makes (or loses) money, understanding the ad business gives the ad man a better understanding of any client's business.

4. Money is made (or lost) in relation to the sum of the efficiency of these three parts: (1) buying, (2) manufacturing or processing, (3) selling.

5. An advertising agency makes money by the efficiency with which it buys materials and services for its operations and for use in clients' campaigns; by the efficiency with which it produces campaigns; by the price at which it sells its services.

6. A "job ticket" system is used for noncommissionable work.
   A "total time" system is used for commissionable work.

7. Three *direct costs* in agency operation may be selected from the following: (1) formal research, (2) comprehensive layout or design, (3) mechanicals, (4) art and photography, (5) photo direction, (6) talent and models, (7) creative fee, (8) publicity, (9) music, (10) product management, (11) production travel and expenses.

   Three *indirect costs* are included here: (1) rent, (2) general administration, (3) corporate finances, (4) accounting, (5) media buying and scheduling, (6) client service, (7) copy and plans, (8) traffic, (9) secretarial and clerical, (10) employee training, (11) nonexpensed travel, (12) phone, (13) postage.

Indirect costs are recovered by the markup on direct costs in billing job tickets and commissions earned from media.

8. The ad man who aspires to management responsibility in the agency should be proficient in: (1) the creation of effective advertising; (2) client service and new business acquisitions; (3) the selection, training, and development of employees; (4) the management of the money.

9. A man will do his best work when his special talents and interests are recognized and encouraged; this means fitting the job to the man, not the man to the job.

10. Four common sense rules for management of the money are as follows: (1) don't spend more than you take in; (2) pay your bills promptly; insist that clients pay you promptly; (3) keep general overhead expenses down; (4) pay your employees well and fairly.

CHAPTER FIFTEEN: USEFUL INFORMATION

1. A "trade" name refers to the name of the manufacturer. A "brand" name refers to the product's specific name; it gives the product an identity within its generic classification, and sets it apart from other products in the manufacturer's family.

2. There are 52 classifications for goods, and 8 classifications for services.

3. The basic legal requirements for the use of a trademark are:

1) It must be placed physically on the product or its container (this includes tags or labels attached to the product and any point-of-sale pieces used with the product).

2) The product must be sold or transported in interstate commerce.

3) The trademark shall not be similar to a competitive product's trademark in appearance, sound, or meaning.

4) The trademark shall not be descriptive or misleading.

5) The trademark shall not be a common surname.

6) The trademark shall not be in poor taste or contrary to public policy.

7) The symbol ® shall be used with the registered trademark.

4. 1. (d)
   2. (f)
   3. (a)
   4. (h)
   5. (b)
   6. (c)
   7. (g)
   8. (e)
   9. (i)

5. 1. (d)
   2. (e)
   3. (g)
   4. (h)
   5. (b)
   6. (c)
   7. (a)
   8. (f)
   9. (i)

6. The markup on cost will be 50%. The selling price will then yield a 33-1/3% margin.

7. Furniture stores, on the average, mark up *100%* to yield a 50% margin on retail price.

A food product is marked up *25%* to yield a 20% margin on retail price.

Automotive wholesalers mark up *40%* to yield a 28-1/2% margin on retail price.

An advertising agency marks up *17.65%* to yield a 15% margin on retail price.

8.　　　ℒ／　　take out character indicated

　　　　━━━　　(underscore): italicize

　　　　∿∿∿　　(underscore): bold face

　　　　ℐ　　　start paragraph

　　　　⌒　　　close up

　　　　#　　　space

　　　　]⌈　　　center copy

Index